Martha's Mandala:

Figures in a Family Circle

Martha Oliver-Smith

SPUYTEN DUYVIL
New York City

Aknowledgments

For their help, support and encouragement over the years it has taken me to research, remember and write this story, I would like to thank the following people: my husband, Stephen Pitkin, for his kindness, humor, patience, and total support; my children, Michael, Caitlin, Alysoun, and Jack for being wonderful cheerleaders; my brother Tony and sister Pippa for sharing the artwork, helping me remember our childhood, and for being such an important part of MayMay's story—our story. I am also very grateful to the all the writing women in my life, but in particular: Terrie Martin, Rita Grauer, Pat Miller, and Peggy Sapphire all of whom have read my work and shared their own writing with me over the years. Many thanks to my friend Kathleen Parvin whose enthusiastic and professional editorial assistance has been essential; to my daughter Caitlin Quinby (again) who read the manuscript with great care and a professional eye; to Laura Kalpakian who encouraged me many years ago and kept reminding me to write this story; to Rachel Hadas, who said "come to New York and do a reading," and to Sue William Silverman, adviser, mentor and friend in the writing program at Vermont College of Fine Arts where I wrote the first of many drafts.

Library of Congress Cataloging-in-Publication Data

Oliver-Smith, Martha, 1917-1981.
  Martha's mandala : figures in a family circle / Martha Oliver-Smith.
    pages cm
  ISBN 978-0-9661242-8-6
  1. Jungian psychology. 2. Psychoanalysis. 3. Bacon, Leonard, 1887-1954. 4.
Oliver-Smith, Martha, 1917-1981. 5. Jung, C. G. (Carl Gustav), 1875-1961. I.
Title.
  BF173.5.O55 2014
  150.19'54092--dc23
                    2014009458

For my grandmother, the artist, Martha Stringham Bacon

Introduction: First Circle

My grandmother, MayMay, as we call her, hides her drawings and paintings in a small room tucked under the eaves of the attic in her house. Some are stacked on a large table or stashed in portfolios leaning against the walls. A Japanese Tansu chest holds palettes and tin boxes of dried-up watercolor paints, layers of yellowing paper, and brushes of all sizes with bristles now sparse and splayed. An easel stands waiting in shafts of dust motes by a window that looks down on the fields behind the house. MayMay has not painted or drawn anything for years, not since my grandfather died in 1954.

She leads me up the three flights of stairs to her studio on the morning of my wedding. I am eighteen and pregnant, terrified and yet triumphant that I have caused much consternation and embarrassment to my mother and stepfather. Mine will be the first shotgun wedding in all the generations of this family of properly raised and educated men and women. The consequences of the heedless way I have managed to get out from under what I consider extreme parental tyranny have only just begun to dawn on me: marriage to a boy I've known for one semester, my education side-lined, no income, a baby due in early March. My young husband to be and I are both still in college—I've only just finished my freshman year, not very successfully—but this "situation" in 1965 requires us to marry so my mother and stepfather can save face—as I see it.

I am afraid but ready to escape, to have my own life. I believe the life I'll have will be my own life because the baby is still a romantic notion. As an eighteen-year-old English major, I have few to no domestic or marketable skills and no idea of how to manage money. All I know is that I will be leaving The Acorns, the home that had always been a sanctuary until my mother's third husband moved in several months ago.

I am familiar with the attic room and its contents, having spent hours here as a young child. My grandmother showed all of us—my brother and sister and me—her watercolors and drawings, illustrations for children's stories she had written and read to us, portraits of family and friends, sketches of landscapes, and versions of her finished mandalas. This morning in the midst of the chaotic preparations for the hastily planned wedding, she has taken me aside.

Almost silent for the past few months, MayMay has been watching, enduring the battle of wills in the house, some of them silent skirmishes, some of them briefly loud—a single bullet bark from my stepfather putting an argument to death. It has been ages since I have taken time to stop and acknowledge her with more than a quick hello and a kiss. MayMay, always small and fragile, seems more frail than usual. She is pale, unsteady on her feet, clearly unwell. Living in this house taken over by my mother and her new husband, a stuffy and rigid retired British army officer, has taken its toll on all of us, but my grandmother's surrender to the force of their combined wills has diminished her almost to the point of invisibility.

Now, however, she wants to know what I would like for a wedding present. Some protective daemon speaks for me before I can think to request a toaster or a baby crib. The answer comes to me without a conscious thought:

"A painting. I want one of your paintings."

At first she shakes her head. "They're no good." And then, after a pause, "Why would you want one?"

It seems obvious to me. The paintings are beautiful; they are part of my childhood landscape, but I can't find the words to explain. Finally, I tell her that I just want to have one of her paintings so I can look at it every day.

When she asks which one, I request the large black and white one of seven star clusters shaped like hearts arced in a semi-circle around a woman reclining in dark space. The fine lines of the woman's figure and the stars are drawn in white ink on the black background. But MayMay tells me, "No. I can't give this one away—it is one of my visions."

Though disappointed, I don't try to persuade her. For someone usually so accommodating, her response is clear and firm. Instead I ask her to choose the one she thinks I should have. She stands still for a few moments before she pulls out a large watercolor from among a few framed paintings stacked behind the door—her final mandala. It is one of thirteen she painted in the 1930s, and though I hadn't known it before, exactly the one I want. I have always loved its bold yet finely painted concentric circles with two green rivers flowing across them to meet at the center as they flow out to the four corners of the picture.

She explains the imagery detailed into its pale green underwater light, its ghostly architectural structures, and the rings of blue and rose-pink filled with diaphanous male and female figures. These are my grandmother's people and dwellings. In the foreground below the circles, a tiny figure stands on heavy boulders partially submerged under dark blue water. The figure gazes up at the circles, arms outstretched, one raised, the other lowered with the hand open at a narrow hip. An invisible breeze blows the filmy fabric that partially covers the androgynous body. My grandmother tells me this is her creative spirit.

At the center of the innermost circle where the two rivers cross, a white flower, cruciform and stylized, glows, its four petals open and flat, pistils and stamens so minute they look at first glance like the folds of a navel. Surrounding the flower are her most important symbols: a three-masted sailing ship, an arrow, a Pegasus, a chalice, a glistening starry jewel (the same as the jewels in the black star cluster painting), a butterfly, a dove, a rose, a Christ child.

I cannot identify the flower as a particular species, but it could be the dogwood bloom—a symbol of Christian sacrifice. I think my grandmother would not have described it as such, nor was she religious in the conventional sense. I have no memory of her ever going to church. While the symbols are archetypal, they are also very personal.

I wish I could remember all that she told me of her images. At eighteen, I didn't think to write down what each one stood for, nor did I recognize at the time that my grandmother's wedding present came with certain responsibilities. I knew I would always care for the painting, but I had to learn how to use it for its intended purpose. The final task, which I would come to understand as I grew older, was a compelling desire to discover the mandala's story and to complete the task of telling that story. Perhaps because we share the same name, Martha, and the same nickname, Patty, she designated me for the role with the faith that I, in spite of my inauspicious launch into the adult world, would come around to fulfilling the task.

Her story would gestate within me for more than forty years before I could begin to tell it in writing. It would take an abrupt and painful change in my familiar world to start the process. One night in February of 2001, my second husband announced without warning that he was leaving the marriage. We had been together for twenty-five years, but there would be no discussion, no explanation. He was done. Too stunned to speak or move, I remember only a sense of total disconnection from my regular world. I felt as if I'd been shot into outer space.

By the time of my husband's defection, I was spinning in place and avoiding the issues. Since my children were grown and out in the world, I could not use them as an excuse to pretend that everything was fine. I had been complacent about my life and resigned to the notion that being miserable in a marriage and stagnant in my work was just the way my life was. Though still committed to my work as a high school English teacher, I felt stultified by the drudgery of toiling in an educational system mired in the politics of testing and fears of litigation. I longed to start working "someday" on my writing, but whenever I considered the possibility of writing, two voices—one timid, one insidious, both insistent—argued in my head. The timid one wanted me to write. I even listened to it sometimes. I had actually written a few poems and an article that were published in small journals. But my efforts were tentative and erratic, with little to show for my literary yearnings. The other voice told me that I would never be a writer. It reminded me every time I had an urge to write a poem that I didn't want to be like my mother who had been a writer, a poet and novelist. My grandfather had been a successful writer too, and I couldn't compete with either of them. That was the stronger voice. It was no use for me to write. I would never be good enough or have the determination to follow through. I would just live with the way things were because I was lazy and lacked the courage to change.

On the night my husband announced that he was "done," I was in shock—reeling at the sudden unraveling of the worn-out fabric of my life as I knew it. In retrospect, what happened and the way it happened was inevitable and shouldn't have been a surprise, but at the time the events felt cataclysmic. That night after my husband left, I found myself sitting in a dark living room, my mind careening in disbelief at the alteration in my known world. At some point during my stunned paralysis, I looked up to see a shaft of light from the hallway reflecting off the glass on the frame of my grandmother's mandala where it hung on the living room wall.

Propelled from my chair, I got up and turned on a light so I could look at the painting closely for the first time in years. I stared at the swirl of circles, the crossed rivers, colors and figures— my grandmother's illustrated universe and the stories within it that were from my world—because they were her world. She had raised me, taught me, and given me this painting that now both comforted and confronted me. Even in the midst of this painful experience, I understood that I was at the end and the beginning of a cycle, that though it would take time, I would heal and move forward with what I had to do.

Soon after that night, I had a dream. I was on a beautiful beach under a warm sun in a bright blue sky. The sand

MSB, *Martha's Mandala*, c. 1940s.

was white and smooth, the water very clear, calm, and turquoise, like a poster for a Caribbean resort. I waded into the warm sea up to my knees and looked down to see hundreds of jigsaw puzzle pieces shimmering below the water's surface on the sand. I began to pick up the multi-colored pieces very carefully, spreading them along the length of my arms to bring them back to shore where I set them down on the beach. I went back and forth between the water and the beach several times, knowing that I had to get all the pieces to the beach so that I could then put the whole puzzle together.

The dream was clear to me immediately. As soon as I could make it happen—now, not "someday"—I had to discover the story of the mandala and how it came to be. It was time to figure out why, at this time of my life, I found myself floating in outer space with two failed marriages and an inner battle between desire and fear that kept me from telling that story.

Within a year I would quit my job, find a new one, sell my house, and move across the country from Oregon to Vermont. There I began the long process of researching, learning and writing my grandmother's story in order to comprehend the beginnings of my own. It has taken more than ten years to write the story. I still had to make a living and open myself to all the new experiences that come with sudden change, but the story has found its way out of the stacks and piles of journals, letters, and essays, the lost and found paintings, out of memory and imagination and, at last, onto the page.

The mandala hangs in my office in my home on the outskirts of a rural village in Vermont, a permanent fixture in my life, always in a place where I can easily see it. I study it—stare at the pulsating circle, which at times appears to be an eye—or a womb. The marriage for which it was a gift is long over, my grandmother's house has been sold several times in the intervening years, and my oldest child, now a grown man in his forties, has his own interesting life on the opposite side of the country. But the mandala serves the purpose for which my grandmother imagined it. She described this purpose in a formal essay written in 1961:

> …..*For having made a mandala, I found that I would often look at it and let it do the acting. So—what good does that do? In case that is a question to ask. The answer is—none at all, unless there truly comes from it an ingathering of strength that might give impetus to the helping hand at times when it is reaching toward an immediate need. I was attuned to a dark thinking that resulted in a melting and breaking, fathoms down, of the featureless mosaic of day-to-day experience, and almost accidentally learned that I could participate in the re-creation of that unquiet jumble and help to give it sunlight, symmetry, and order.*[1]

Whether I am at peace or in times of stress, I find that spending time with the mandala always provides a way to some understanding or solace. The painting originated from a dream that came out of my grandmother's darkness; it is the re-creation of her fractured psyche transformed through the assembled elements of her mysterious images, use of color, light, order and symmetry to heal the "dark-thinking" of her unquiet mind. Carl Jung wrote in *Modern Man in Search of a Soul*, "A great work of art is like a dream; for all its apparent obviousness it does not explain itself and is never unequivocal.[2] My grandmother would have argued that her painting was not a great work of art, but it is indeed a fine mandala, one that tells a story filled with ambiguities that elude an explanation.

MSB, *Rose Mandala*, c. 1934; courtesy of David Davis.

I
FAMILY CIRCLES

*S*tories are like wheels, and so are unborn creatures in the womb.
They begin as a little center of intensity where they whirl and whirl,
gathering about themselves their beginnings and their endings. …
The child's beginning and center has an intensity beyond our knowing,
and all that is to be, is slowly gathered to it, including bit by bit, and
most illogically—the skeleton, while the blood goes round and round.
Stories and wheels and children and time—or a nebula, or a rose—what
have they to do with one another? … Call it analogy, metaphor, parable,
coincidence, or a Pierian spring, it hides itself (though it is in plain sight)
as if not to weary us. It never importunes, though it seems to entreat, and
it is never to be sought, though it may be discerned. [3]

My grandmother's words about stories suggest that in telling her story I will be
telling my own, that in doing so I should follow the circle of the turning wheel—the
story's vehicle "gathering about [itself] its beginnings and endings." Martha Stringham
Bacon's story is a tale of madness and art, of poetry and painting, of psychoanalysis and
spirituality inhabited by characters real and imagined, grand and humble. Its people,
places and metaphors go around and around, "entreating" to be reborn until it comes
around to me to tell it through the written words of the characters, my own childhood
memories of my grandparents, and my imagination.

The particular "story" my grandmother referred to in her journal began with
madness—a sudden assault on the senses—strange and violent voices that seemed
to come out of nowhere, causing the wheel on its regular path to veer off course so
that she lost her bearings entirely. Throughout her life she would attempt to explain
what she would call the "tidal wave" that took over her life and nearly drowned her

in 1922. Through her paintings and writing, she would tell and re-tell the story of her experience in an imagined universe that called to her first in seductive whispers and then in horrifying voices. The voices were in her head but separated her from her accustomed life in the "outside," real world of her family and daily life. She would return to the world, at first with great effort and regret, but then willingly and with gratitude always tinged with longing for that other place where her creative spirit continued to live in exile.

But the madness is only one revolution of the story's turning wheel. Somewhere between its beginnings, the madness, and whatever its ending might be, there is the circumference of a circle, the outer rim that contains and even holds the center and its contents in place. From there the spiral moves inward. The creative minds and spirits of two men, my grandfather, Leonard Bacon, and Dr. Carl Jung, each in his own way formed the sphere of Martha Stringham Bacon's life as a woman and an artist. As I follow the images that coil toward the center—the self she sought to hold—I see that my grandfather's universe enveloped hers, while Dr. Carl Jung's theories of the psyche suffused her spiritual worldview as both structured her life.

MSB, *Small Sketches Series*, 1940s.

My grandparents' stories are intertwined, but my grandfather's was the dominant strand in the fabric of their lives. Leonard Bacon's universe was expansive and, though devoted to his art, it was of this world. His personality and way of life overshadowed my grandmother's. Born in 1887 to the wealthy upper class, he lived in a privileged world. On his father's side, the Bacons were an old New Haven family of ministers, academics and successful businessmen. Leonard's father, Nathaniel Terry Bacon, was a scientist, engineer and scholar, who with Rowland G. Hazard, another rich aristocrat, helped to develop the Solvay Process Company in America, eventually leading to the founding of Allied Chemical Corporation. Nathaniel Bacon worked for Rowland Hazard and then married his boss's daughter, Helen Hazard, settling in Peace Dale, Rhode Island where the Hazards also owned the textile mills that supported the town.

To his father's dismay, Leonard showed no interest or aptitude for the family businesses; instead, after finishing college at Yale in the Bacon family tradition, he gravitated to the arts. He knew he wanted "to write poetry and nothing but poetry,"[4] as he proclaimed in his autobiography *Semi-Centennial*. His father did not have much use for poetry as a profession and attempted to launch Leonard into several manly and conventional careers. These included managing a failing family-owned rubber plantation in Nicaragua, toiling on a dude ranch in Montana, and working as a secretary and assistant to the manager of an Alabama cotton plantation. None of these labors appealed, but Leonard endured them for his father's sake until he was offered a teaching position at the University of California at Berkeley, paving his way to become a poet, translator and literary critic.

At the beginning of *Semi-Centennial*, Leonard quotes Chekhov: "It is pleasant to be even a small author," which is what my grandfather was. He published many works of poetry, literary criticism and translations of works in German, Italian, Spanish, French, and Portuguese. A gregarious public figure in literary circles of the time, he was inducted into the American Academy of Arts and Letters and won the Pulitzer Prize for poetry in 1941. He published eight volumes of formal verse, as well as a translation in 1945 of the epic poem *The Lusiads* by the 16th century Portuguese poet Camoes, still considered one of the finest English translations of the work. Published in 1939, *Semi-Centennial,* an acknowledgment of turning fifty and subtitled *The Life and Some of the Opinions of Leonard Bacon*, is just that, an engaging volume of humorous egoism about his life and literary adventures with interesting people he encountered. Perhaps in deference to my grandmother's sense of privacy, my grandfather omitted her almost entirely from the book, though he dedicated it to her and his daughters. He briefly mentions her perhaps three times—and never by name—referring to her once as "The Lady in question" while describing their wedding engagement.

Though less financially substantial than the Bacon/Hazards, my grandmother came from similar New Haven roots through her mother's family, the Days. The Days, like the Bacons, were scientists, engineers and academics (a great grandfather, Jeremiah Day, was a president of Yale from 1817-1846), who as part of the westward expansion movement migrated to California to teach subsequent generations of the 1849 gold rush. Her father, Irving Stringham, was a mathematician from New York State and a lapsed Mormon who also made his way to California, where he became a professor at the new university in Berkeley. Stringham was the first person to denote the natural logarithm that is commonplace in digital calculators today.[5]

Born in Berkeley, Martha Sherman Stringham was a middle child and younger daughter of three children. Named Martha Sherman for her mother and for an ancestor whose husband, Roger Sherman, signed the Declaration of Independence, she was nicknamed Patty, another tradition of the "Marthas" in the Day family. Quiet, small, pretty and very bright, she was educated at the Anna Head School in Berkeley (now the Head Royce School), a progressive school for girls that gave her a fine education. She was not formally trained as an artist but did take drawing classes after she graduated from high school. Though her family's roots were in the east, she considered herself a native Californian. Re-transplanted to the east coast by marriage, she never stopped longing for the west, where she could watch the sun setting into the sea.

My grandparents met when my grandfather was hired for his very first and apparently only official full-time job, teaching English literature and composition at Berkeley. They married in 1912 and began their lives together with every advantage that inherited wealth and education could provide. Entering the second decade of the 20th century, they were full of energy and creativity, open to new ideas, yet bound to certain traditions and values from the previous century. They stayed in Berkeley, where Leonard taught and their three daughters were born, until 1926. At that time they moved back east to Rhode Island, after his parents' deaths within six months of each other, to live at The Acorns.

Patty Bacon, *Engagement Portrait*, c. 1911-12.

The Acorns, c. 1985.

The Acorns is another center that forms this narrative, a locus in real time and space from which the story emanates. One of five in a constellation of houses built by the Bacon/Hazard family, it was called The Acorns because it was a satellite to a much larger and grander place, the Hazard/Bacon mansion, known as Oakwoods. The Hazard family built the five houses for themselves, all within walking distance, though not in sight of one another. The Acorns was a gift to Helen, daughter of Rowland Hazard, in 1882 when she married Nathaniel Terry Bacon.

Four generations of Bacons lived in The Acorns over the course of eighty-four years, but while the main Hazard branch remained active and successful in business, the Bacons lived off their trust funds. They spent their time writing poetry, painting, studying languages, and playing music—none of which produced much financial reward. They lived with such a blithe lack of interest in finances that Leonard was blindsided by the depression in the 1930s. Later, he was burdened by dependent family members and cheated by financial advisors but limped along with his much reduced trust fund until his death in 1954. My grandmother somehow managed to keep the house going on what little remained for another thirteen years.

Until I was an adult, the source from which the money trickled remained a mystery. The family income was never discussed, the subject being more distasteful even than sex, worse than a dirty joke at the dinner table. I grew up with a constant sense of the fluctuating tides of money, an anxiety that always lay just beneath the surface of our daily lives. Still, I remember with great affection the stacks of chipped china in the pantry, peeling plaster, groaning plumbing, the furnace gasping at each exhalation of heat, resuscitated somehow every winter, the series of undependable used cars. The often-repeated phrase "We can't afford it" remains familiar to me as a nursery rhyme refrain.

After my grandmother's death in 1967, my mother and stepfather sold The Acorns for $26,000. Needing a new roof and furnace, complete re-wiring and plumbing as well as new paint and plaster in every room, the place had reached a nadir of disrepair. Its decline had been long and gradual. When I was born in 1946, the family fortunes, especially in our branch of the Hazard clan, were steadily ebbing. I grew up with stories but no real memory of the days when a butler, a cook, housemaids and a full-time gardener and handyman pruned, polished and pampered the family. What remained

The Acorns, c. 1960s.

for my generation, the last to live in the house, was a Victorian museum with no one to guard the rooms and doors or keep children away from the artifacts. We had the run of the place, only gradually growing into consciousness of its decrepitude.

The Acorns was the geographical and emotional center of life for four generations of the Bacon family including my own. Even long after my grandfather's death in 1954, the place seemed to vibrate with his large presence, his books, and clothes—the white spats in old boxes and linen suits that still hung in closets, his bird-calling whistle, the echo of his uproarious laughter as he pounded the dining room table with his beer stein and held forth about poetry, literature and the people he knew.

It was at The Acorns that my grandfather did most of his writing, but he lived a very public and peripatetic life, spending much of his time bouncing around restlessly between New York, Providence, New Haven and Boston, where he had many literary friends and colleagues. He also took off on week-long fishing and hunting trips as well as on long-distance jaunts, sometimes with the family, but often not. In his early years he traveled to Central America and throughout Europe. Later he would take the family to England, France and Italy. In 1928, they moved to Florence where he planned to live permanently as an expatriate writer, joined by Frederick Faust, a friend and former student and his family.[6] The Bacons, however, disillusioned and horrified by the Fascist regime in Italy, returned to Peace Dale in 1932. The entire family loved Florence and always spoke of those years as an idyllic time in their lives. My grandmother wrote and illustrated an account of their life in a Florentine villa and the summer place in Forte de Marme.

Leonard loved to entertain in grand style at home and go to events where he could be center stage. He was famous for holding court, reciting poetry and waxing eloquent late into the night while his guests, worn out with fatigue and quantities of alcohol,

MSB,
The Bacon daughters:
Helen (top),
Marnie (center),
Alice,
Florence Series:
c. 1928 -32.

felt obliged to wait him out. He was also devoted to fishing and bird watching in the once rural Rhode Island community known as "South County," the subject and setting of many of his poems. Despite all his peregrinations, he found time to write; there was no question that his work and his art took precedence over all other concerns by divine right.

Patty Bacon, unlike her husband, was intensely shy. She wrote in her journals about her dread of the social obligations attached to Leonard's growing celebrity. Within my grandfather's universe, she conformed and functioned as the traditional "Angel of the House," but in her few stolen private hours, she was a woman striving to discover her center as an artist. On the rare occasions that she wasn't tending to the many demands of her family and running a large house, my grandmother would quietly disappear into her small attic studio to draw and paint. She was Leonard's wife and mother of his three daughters, but she created a separate and private universe for herself within that family sphere, seeking a way to fulfill herself through painting and writing. In a letter to her middle daughter, Helen Bacon, in 1949, she wrote of her life-long compulsion:

...if you could hear me clattering up and down and up and down and up and downstairs because I am doing one thing up in the attic and twenty-five in the other parts of the house, it would seem as if little was going on. I am sloshing around with paints, and if I should actually produce something that could be called a picture, that would be news I suppose. However, I am not too optimistic about that, so why do I do it? God knows—only this is certain, that it is a drive toward no result, but anyhow a drive, and appearances to the contrary—it has always been there, in spite of gigantic interruptions lasting sometimes five or eight years. Age and other limitations haven't put an end to it yet.[7]

MSB, *Cartoon Series*
(San Carlos Hotel). New York, 1941.

My grandmother also wrote personal journals, essays and children's stories, many of which she illustrated; she worked on a number of versions of a novel-length story for years. It was a Jungian hero's journey that retold the story of her illness symbolically, a story that she was never satisfied with, nor would ever finish. She wrote a factual record, what she called a "case history," of her experience with madness as well, but it was the thirteen drafts of the long story that she struggled to write for most of her life. Her paintings and writing reveal her inner life, and a striving to express herself in a world that she often found overwhelming. Reserved and self-effacing, Patty Bacon craved invisibility, solitude, and unfettered time, very little of which she had.

Though they were devoted to and dependent on each other, my grandparents spun in their own orbits, each hindered in his and her own way by individual psychological conflicts. In temperament and personality, my grandparents, as Dr. Carl Jung might say, were a "pair of opposites": Leonard was the irrepressible extrovert, and Patty a profound introvert. Though both were artists, he was acknowledged in a literary world that first embraced then rejected him; she, on the other hand, retreated not only into the world of domesticity but deep within herself, in spite of a longing for recognition she never received from the larger world.

Dr. Carl Jung appears in person at the outer rim of the Bacon family story from 1925 into the late '40s, but his ideas, philosophies, professional and personal relations were at the core of Bacon family values, informing and shaping my grandparents' lives and those of the following generations. The Bacons devoutly espoused Jung's theories of the human psyche as the primary rationale and remedy for their anxieties, fears, physical symptoms, dreams and desires; they were also charmed by his magnetism, readily joining the ranks of other wealthy American devotees. As I grew up in this family for whom Jung's theories about the human psyche were almost a religion, I never questioned the gospel of his message. His aura was a persistent presence, drifting through the house in daily conversations. Everyone shared dreams at the breakfast table and discussed the family complexes over cocktails. Nervous breakdowns were not uncommon, and I remember overhearing intriguing gossip about my mother or certain aunts and cousins—grown-ups who were in various states of emotional disarray.

Jung's terminology pervaded my grandfather's poems and flew in letters to and from Zurich. My grandmother, a prodigious dreamer, filled notebooks describing her nightly visions. Because I spent most of my childhood living in my grandparents' house, I remember listening, as if learning my catechism, to explanations of archetypes, the collective unconscious, pairs of opposites, the anima and animus, synchronicity. Was I an extrovert or an introvert? I often wondered as I grew up in this family so influenced by Jung's ideas.

Jung came into the Bacon's lives out of necessity. He was my grandfather's savior. In 1923 Leonard was able to quit his teaching job and support the family on the capacious Hazard trust fund. Released from the servitude of teaching freshman composition and grading papers, he at first felt liberated and settled into his role as gentleman poet. Between 1923 and 1925, he published two books of poetry and had started a third, but during this time he began to suffer from a "melancholia—which descended upon me like a cloud....I was perfectly married, I had three lovely children, I had enough money for our modest necessities...."[8] Urged by his Santa Barbara friends, Chauncey and Henriette Goodrich, who were already well established in Jung's American coterie, to seek counsel with Dr. Jung, Leonard at first resisted, believing the whole concept of psychoanalysis to be an exercise in futility: "The more depressed I became the more intransigent I grew with respect to all that rigmarole, which I felt compared with phrenology and homeopathy. To me it was witch-doctoring."[9] But his internal misery persisted and finally he relented. He traveled overseas to Zurich several times to attend Jung's seminars and undergo psychoanalytic sessions with Toni Wolff.

In the autobiography, my grandfather wrote about his first session:

"I don't think there is any relief in the world comparable to the first expectoration of your griefs. In my case it was so immediate that I was actually able to grin feebly when Miss

Zurich, 1925 or 1927.
Back left: Leonard Bacon;
Dr. Carl Jung; Peter Baynes.
Front: Paul Radin. Courtesy of Leonard
Bacon Archives, Beinecke Library.

W __ after reviewing my collection of inner horror said with pardonable irony: All this seems pretty infantile."[10] After the euphoria of the first session passed, he wrote to the Goodriches:

"[Your letter] caught me heavily engaged. The barrage is coming down, all my aeroplanes have been shot down, and the whole sector is active. I have in short been in Hell for 24 hours. I have paid several long visits in Malebolge, and know all the most distinguished citizens."[11]

During that time, it appears that post-session social gatherings made up for the hard work and his dark nights of the soul in Malebolge (Dante's 8th circle). In the same letter to the Goodriches, Leonard described an evening out with a gang of Jungians:

"[It] was a wonderful party. The Jungs, Cary, Toni Wolff, Provot and I ... went out to Kusnacht and danced all night. Everybody was lit, and Jung was a lively image of Dionysus. It was a sweet party."

The social gatherings clearly alleviated the pain of analysis. As a result of his excruciating analytical sessions, Leonard's melancholia seems to have been cured; he apparently never suffered the affliction again. While still in Zurich he began to write the poems that appear in *Animula Vagula,* which he referred to as his "Saison en Enfer." Fifteen years later he would write "Analytical Dictionary" (later titled "Mnemonic System for Psycho-analysts" for publication), a whimsical, humorous poem describing Jung's universe in Zurich that follows the alphabet from A to Z:

> Analytical Dictionary
>
> A is for Anima playing a role
> A trifle obscure in the masculine soul.
> B is for Beckwith who poses God knows.
> C is for Cary who knows it's a pose.
> D is for Dream, I must say in effect,
> Whose meaning you never are led to suspect.
> E is for extrovert, finest that lives,
> Whom the introvert neither forgets nor forgives.
> F is for Freud who invented analysis,
> And also for fantasy, feeling and fallacies.
> G is for gabble emitted by Schmitz
> Who bungled the points and excited the wits.

H is hypothesis, daring as Hell,
That no one but Jung understands very well.
I is for introvert taking a ride,
In a squirrel cage hung in his little inside.
J is for Jung who perpetually plots
A new process for tying my soul into knots.
K is the Klatch, roving there roving here,
When the Seminar's done in an ocean of beer.
L is libido that surges and rolls
In furious streams through remarkable souls.
M is for mana—it's one of my curses
That somehow I can't get it into my verses.
N is for "Neurot"—I'll mention to you
That the rot is quite rotten, and the new isn't new.
O is for opposites yoked in a pair,
P is for psychology, not that I care!
Q is the quibble that started much quacking
When reasonable themes for discussion were lacking.
R is for Radin who tied without fail,
Anthropology's can to Psychology's tail.
S is for seminar sitting quite tight,
While Grandfather rises from height unto height.
T is the tempest all passion revealing,
when anyone raises the subject of feeling.
U is the Unbewusst under us all
Where animae whimper and animi brawl.
V is volubility, trait atavistic,
Which, I think, is perhaps our chief characteristic.
W is Wolff, who must always deplore
That Bacon and Beckwith once came to her door.
X is the thing that my analyst knows,
But which she can never be brought to disclose.
Y is for Yang. It is also the Yin,
Meaning masculine virtue and feminine sin.

Z is for Zurich, where it is well known,
That far-wandering NUT has come into his own. [12]

The passage of time allowed for the satirical humor of "Analytical Dictionary" while the poems in *Animula Vagula*, composed during and soon after his time in Zurich, are filled with angst and darkness. That he could not (or would not) explain from whence the angst and darkness came seems extremely odd.

It is easy to understand why my grandfather's personality and range of motion in the world eclipsed his wife's small, confined universe. He skirmished with the external forces of the literary world—the critics, the rivals, the changing times and shifting theories on the direction that modern poetry should take. At home though, Leonard was the center of the universe, a benevolent dictator. His wife and daughters adored him though they freely acknowledged his flaws—his prejudices, his drinking, and egotism—but that didn't diminish his role as the beloved patriarch. That he hardly mentions his personal life, especially his family, in the autobiography is a conscious choice that he suggests in the dedication: "To Martha, Helen, Alice, and their Mother, who do not Appear Frequently in these Pages for a Reason Sufficiently Expressed by the Poet Donne."[13]

Leonard's insistence on keeping the autobiography impersonal is quite unsatisfying to today's sensibilities and expectations of titillating personal confessions; readers and audiences are accustomed to celebrities and everyone else revealing too much information about themselves, but my grandfather devotes a whole chapter in *Semi-Centennial* to his time in Zurich, never explaining the nature of his depression. He dismisses not only the readers' curiosity but their capacity to understand his distress. He wrote, "Since nothing on earth could be more boring than such a case-history, I am not going into the details. It would be as dull as a stream of consciousness novel, and not unlike one. And I do not propose to inflict anything like that on a reader who might be capable of even more damaging comparisons."[14] He closes the door on our curiosity with evasive irony by complimenting the reader on his or her good taste to be bored with a case history. In this cantankerous though humorous statement, my grandfather also exposes his obtuse resistance to the formal innovations and new directions developing in the literary world.

What he refuses to reveal is the context of his affliction—the backstory that began in the fall of 1922 when my grandmother suffered a nervous breakdown that lasted well into the following year. The other artist in the family, Patty Bacon, the covert painter and writer, was engaged in a battle for her life, struggling with internal forces that threatened to take over her mind. The whirling story had spun out of control two years before Leonard's depression and three before he went to Zurich for analysis. For all of his agonies in Malebolge, he either did not recognize or refused to acknowledge that his wife's illness may have contributed to his own depression and the ensuing embrace of Jung and psychoanalysis.

Letter from Toni Wolff to Leonard Bacon, April 27, 1934.
Courtesy of Leonard Bacon Archives, Beinecke Library.

II
Center of Intensity:
A Tidal Wave

At the time of my grandmother's breakdown, the family was still in California. Life was full of caring for her children: Martha, called Marnie, age six, Helen, age four, and Alice, who was not quite two. Patty was also helping her widowed mother who lived next door. Her older sister Harriet, a difficult and demanding woman and an alcoholic, also lived there with her twin daughters. Harriet's life was in constant turmoil. Separated from her husband and without reliable income, she was dependent emotionally and financially on my grandparents until her death in 1953. Harriet and her woes added an extra burden to the Bacons' responsibilities.

When she could find the time, Patty Bacon was also trying to be an artist, working on portraits, and landscapes in pen and ink and watercolor. Late in 1922, she began to experience what she later referred to as a "crack-up" and described as a "psychological tidal wave." Thirty years after her breakdown my grandmother wrote a formal essay about this harrowing experience, a sixteen-page account she titled *The Friend in the Unconscious*. Here she describes the sudden change:

> *It was wild weather out of nowhere. I had health, youth, was happily married, had romped though a marvelous childhood, and had never been "neurotic" or a problem as far as anyone, including myself could see. I had recently been through a rather burdened year of strain and unremitting work, but a little overdoing is proverbially less tricky than not enough to do.*

She believed that the tidal wave might have been caused by "the story" that in *her words suddenly took violent possession of me when several of its characters surged upwards from an unconscious that I did not know existed. But they were so vivid and compelling that their completed drama shaped itself with lightening speed. No need to ask, why a story? There is always a story.*

✳

The Acorns: Peace Dale, Rhode Island—1961

I imagine that the early September afternoon is chilly enough for a fire. My grandmother is in the "library." The room was once my grandfather's study, but since his death it has been hers. Having moved the fireplace screen aside, she sits close to the fire on a low wooden stool, so she can easily feed to the flames each sheet of the eighty-page manuscript she holds on her lap. The brittle typing paper curls into ash. Some pages blow apart in small explosions, sending fiery fragments up the chimney; others maintain the form of the paper for several seconds, the black print turning to greasy purple, still visible before words and page collapse into embers beneath the burning logs.

Patty Bacon is alone in the house. Everyone is reliably out this afternoon shopping for school clothes. As she burns the pages of her manuscript, she treasures the quiet. Once again she has lost her solitude to a houseful of children. My mother, brother, sister and I are back at The Acorns again in the aftermath of my mother's second divorce. We had been living in New York while my mother worked as a fashion magazine copy editor, first for *Vogue* and then *Harper's Bazaar* until my stepfather disintegrated into an alcoholic disaster.

We children are happy going to the local public school and love the freedom to ramble around town on our bicycles or roam the woods near the house with our friends. My mother is not so happy with the situation. She hated leaving the city and having to come "home," but she has settled in to writing her third novel and taking on freelance work—book reviews and articles for *American Heritage Magazine* about women in early American history. These bring in a little money while my grandmother supports us.

Most afternoons, Patty Bacon sits surrounded by the walls of books, on a worn brown plush chaise-lounge facing the corner fireplace. Here she spends her time writing, typing on a big, black Royal typewriter propped on a spindly gray metal table.

I am afraid you children have had too many good things,

and that is why

you are getting so particular

MSB, *Florence Series*, c. 1928-32.

When she tires of working, she lies back, wrapped in an old blue afghan and dozes among the folders and papers strewn about the chaise. She uses Leonard's heavy walnut desk in the back of the room only when she must deal with the Byzantine economics of a dwindling trust fund, the constant financial demands of the disintegrating house, the most recent second-hand car, the ancient furnace in the basement, and her eldest daughter's three growing children.

When Leonard brought the family back to Peace Dale and The Acorns after his parents died in 1926, it became Patty's job to manage the place. It was more work than she could keep up with. She was homesick for the pace and culture of Berkeley, where she grew up, for the soft ochre hills and the Bay, for the west coast. At first the interminable gray Rhode Island winters in the big, drafty house almost overwhelmed her. The voices that she thought she'd conquered sometimes taunted and nagged. Darkness suffused The Acorns in the heavy brown velvet curtains, the wing chairs and sofas upholstered in crimson brocade, all profusely draped with crocheted antimacassars. A stuffed parrot that glowered from a stand in a corner of the parlor completed the sonorous mood of oppressive propriety left over from the previous century. Patty wanted light and air. She pulled down all the velvet and brocade, had the walls painted the color of thick cream, re-covered furniture in lighter shades and fabrics, and banished the parrot to the attic to be eaten by moths. It was not California, but she made The Acorns a place where she could breathe the air and let in the light.

The house was always home base through the times when she and Leonard traveled from one coast to another and spent four years in Florence and a year in Paris. During the war they'd lived in New York or Boston, then moved back and forth between Santa Barbara and The Acorns. It had been a restless life. Since Leonard's death, the place is her permanent home, and she will never again leave it to live anywhere else. Disheveled and ramshackle as the house has become over the years, it is where she belongs. Here, as her daughters went off to school, she found the peace of mind and even some time to paint and write. She has done no painting since Leonard died though; she hasn't had the heart for it, nor will her arthritic hands perform the fine curves and lines required to create the images.

She shakes off the lapse of attention to the task of the moment, concentrating now as the fire consumes the manuscript; nobody will interrupt or question the sacrificial burning of the story—this factual account. These smoldering words are the hard facts that she wrote eight years after the episode when she experienced "the wrong relations of two realities resulting in delusion—"the crack-up," "the tidal wave" as she thinks of it now. All the details, the voices and what they said to her, rise and swirl with the smoke up the chimney to disappear into the air where the wind will erase them forever.

The "facts," the case history of what happened forty years before, will be lost, forgotten. She will write a new piece, a new version that will tell the story as she understands its truth.

At first, she portrayed the "tidal wave" story through painting her dreams and symbols as a kind of allegorical narrative. Over the years, the images of her "tidal wave" turned into thirteen different mandalas. She filled circles, some small, some large, with star clusters and wings, rivers and mountains to illustrate the path of her experience from madness to self-integration. The "story" evolved into something like a novel about the characters that sometimes still murmur, like a pale chorus, in the background sounds of her days. As the fire flares with each page, she thinks perhaps this act of immolation will still the last voice once and for all.

When the voices first came to her in 1922, she was thirty. Her children were very small, all three girls under the age of six. They were living in Berkeley then; Leonard was teaching full time and feeling frustrated about his writing. They had a place at the edge of campus next door to the house where she grew up. It was a solid California bungalow

MSB, *Florence Series*, c. 1928-32.

Bacon Family Portrait: 1922, just prior to the "tidal wave."
Front row L to R: Marnie and Helen Bacon, Margaret Keith.
Back Row: Susan Bacon Keith with infant Nancy; Patty Bacon,
Leonard Bacon, Helen Hazard Bacon and Nathaniel Terry Bacon
holding Alice Bacon.

with deep eaves, cool dark rooms and hardwood floors. The garden was the best part of it, full of jasmine, camellia bushes, a flowering mulberry and a lemon tree, all enclosed by a redwood fence. There were shady places to sit and enough laurel hedge for the children to hide in. Patty could sit outside and draw while keeping an eye on them.

But sometimes she felt overwhelmed dealing with the children, trying to meet Leonard's needs, while also helping her widowed mother who wasn't well, and Harriet who constantly demanded attention. That's when she had begun to think and write a story— what became *the* story. She felt that she was not a writer, had no claim to be a writer, yet the characters of the story compelled her. She even told Leonard, who *was* a writer, as they lay in bed together one night in each other's arms. He was interested, sympathetic, encouraged her to write it down, which she did, a little at a time when she could find a few quiet moments.

Soon, however, the people of the story seemed irresistibly alive, even audible. They whispered at first, words run together, indistinguishable and muffled. But a word or phrase would emerge, a low-pitched laugh. They charmed her, asked favors of her.

She knew she had yielded to the story's characters, even encouraged them, unaware of the danger. At family dinners, she would find herself slipping away, though still seated at the table, listening to their voices and losing the thread of conversations around her. One voice told her about the door in a mountain under the waters of a river. Or she would stop in the middle of bathing a child to summon a presence, a beautiful epicene figure—was it male or female?—whose tenor/alto voice sang to her. Only the piercing shriek of a daughter with soap stinging her eyes would distract her from following the music.

It wasn't long before these characters became a demanding chorus with voices like crows and quarreling jays. They called to her and to each other, sometimes whispering cruel, violent things. Only one soft voice—a woman's—tried to turn back the "tidal wave." Somewhere beneath the cacophony, she could hear a whispered counterpoint: "Peril, peril, peril!" But it was too late. She was lost, almost without resistance, in their universe as if she had fallen into the curl of the wave, pulled back from the shore, tumbling into the sea.

She never actually harmed anyone, though she was not herself, her own self—not Leonard's wife, nor her children's mother. Someone—one of the women in the chorus—perhaps the one who sometimes softly whispered "peril," walked and talked for her. She, not Patty, presided over making beds, being sure to change the sheets each week. She picked up after the children, taught them manners, made sure they ate their vegetables. It was her voice that sang French lullabies when she tucked them in at night. This "other" served tea with thin slices of lemon in gold-rimmed teacups to visiting ladies at four o'clock on Sunday afternoons. She presided over dinners with Leonard's colleagues from the English department when the talk went on into the night. Without complaint, this competent woman directed the maid, conferred with the cook, kept social engagements; wrote thank you notes, did errands, shared Leonard's bed. She, herself, did not sleep, tasted nothing if she ate at all. Her only quiet moments came when she stole time to draw late at night or early in the morning when everyone was asleep.

She was exhausted, but she needed to visualize these people from the sound of their voices, their eyes, torsos, toes, hair. Hylas—he was the hero, Beatrix the princess, and golden-haired Sophie who hid from Beatrix. There was Leo, a dark, angry boy, and The Sylph in his/her fluttering rags. Only in the drawing, shading and posing of these figures was her mind quiet.

Had none of the people around her noticed what was going on? Not her mother, not Leonard, not all the faces and bodies who passed through her daily life? Sometimes she thought she could hear her own, old voice calling out "I'm drowning!" But no sounds emerged from her lips, which strained to make words.

One afternoon, after three days of rain with the children indoors, Patty was helping Marnie and Helen make paper dolls, two princesses, from a story in *The Blue Fairy Book*: Rose Red with long black hair, and Rose White with gold. She had drawn and painted them with watercolors according to the girls' directions, but they were her beautiful paper dolls. Rose Red's dark eyes, smiled, her black tresses unfettered around her face and shoulders, contrasting with her pale skin and delicate, pink cheeks. She wore a light, filmy tunic. A long, red ribbon sash at her waist fluttered as if blown by a breeze. Rose Red now lay on the table, waiting for her paint to dry so she could be cut away from the paper. Picking up the scissors, Patty fit her thumb and finger firmly in their ornate gold loops molded in the shape of curved wings and the long neck of a crane. They were a present from Leonard, a fanciful gift, one of many for her birthday, accompanied by a poem he'd written about birds. Carefully she began to cut through the paper around the delicate form of Rose White, whose paint was now dry. With her yellow hair and blue eyes, she looked like one of Patty's own girls—a little Botticelli nymph—her tunic decorated with blue ribbons.

Marnie and Helen began to quarrel about who would get which doll. Marnie pulled Helen's hair; Helen pinched Marnie hard on the arm. Alice, the baby, fretful and feverish all day with a cold, climbed onto the table, tipping over a glass full of paint water and soaking brushes. A pool of red liquid spread over the cluttered table, a vermilion tide, moving across the table to cover Rose Red. The voices, restive all afternoon in her head, exploded into a riot, their clamor obliterating the shrieks and wails of the children. Another wail, slow and high, penetrated her aching skull, a terrible voice—was it hers?—with terrible words: "You bloody children, I hate you! Look what you did!"

Another voice howled: "Get rid of them—or leave."

Still another voice—whose was it? "Kill them—those scissors in your hand—do it now."

"Drown them out! Drownthemdrownthem," screamed the voices.

She looked at the long scissors in her hand, blades open like the sharp beak of a crane, then closed them slowly across the thin white neck—slashing, metallic bird notes—like a jay's cry. Paper feathers drifted and spiraled in the air, settled in the red pool spreading across the table, landed in the children's hair—Rose White.

Another inconsolable voice moaned at the rising tide that began to fill the room, covering her ankles, knees, hips. How heavy the sea was; she could not move her feet. The scissors fell from her hand, sinking beneath the thick green water to bounce on the patterned rug. Three small, terror-stricken faces floated before her like lopped-off flower heads, blanched white as camellias, as she began to slip under the water, viscous, green, irresistible. Someone came into the room, took her hands, pulled her from the drag of the wave, held her, led her away.

I picture my grandmother, age thirty-one, giving up the struggle to protect her known universe—children, marriage, home—from an assault by beings lying deep inside herself. They ambush her, arriving in the Trojan horse of a story, a gift of seemingly innocent characters wearing benign masks to hide their dark desires. I see her as she lies in a narrow white bed in the small private hospital where she will begin to recover from the "tidal wave." The sheets, white and sterile, are tucked so tightly around her she feels mummified as she listens to the moans and curses of her voices. She cannot move her arms or legs, though she rolls her head from side to side in her distress. These bindings at least seem to keep her parts—her bones and hair, her skin from floating away. Immobilized, Patty dissolves instead within, deep down to a universe beneath the sea, where she sleeps, for hours and days, until she dreams.

A dark chasm like a well seems to be inside of her, miles deep, but she can see the end of it, the faint gleam, not of water, but of moistened earth like garden soil. Out of it blows a small gust of wind—sweet, intoxicating. A clod of earth rolls back to expose the tip of a tight, white bud. The bud grows larger, while another clod moves, crumbles, spraying tiny pellets that scatter down its sides. One immaculate petal gradually frees itself and springs up. In slow motion, it exposes its creamy surface and releases a faint, sweet breath; then another petal unfurls, and another until there are four.

When she wakes, she senses a change. The sheets have come loose; they rest lightly and cool around her as if she has sloughed them off like an old skin. The feeling in the flower dream remains strong within her. She knows it to be a promise of something to guide her through this nightmare—a benign and comforting presence. The image of the white flower pushing through the damp earth at the bottom of the deep well, opening and freeing its essence into the air, calms her. She will later discover the dream-image as a reality again and again. It is not a metaphor, not a concept or a riddle. She will find it in books and in her own paintings. She will explore it and write it all down eventually, but at the moment of waking, the white flower is a mystery.

MSB, *Mere Passing of Minutes,* an illustration for an essay on time. c. 1940s.

I imagine the psychiatrist who interviewed her in the hospital room as a small man, balding like a monk with a tonsure. He might have stood by her bed peering over her in his long white coat and rimless spectacles, murmuring questions: Was she angry with her mother? Did she have nightmares about her father? She would have done her best to answer his questions: No she was not angry with anyone. No she'd had no nightmares, only the voices that told her to do awful things. She had been overcome by the voices.

They told her to kill her children. Had she almost done that? The memory sickened her. She didn't mention her flower dream. The psychiatrist told poor, terrified Leonard that she was suffering from neurasthenia but that she would work through the trouble if she followed Dr. S. Weir Mitchell's Rest Cure for a month or two. This meant she had to rest for days and weeks, with no reading, writing or painting. She had to follow a strict diet of bland, healthy foods and drink lots of milk. The doctor said nothing to her. In fact, he never came back.

She stayed for five weeks in the hospital wrestling with the voices. Never had she been so alone, but the voices receded, dwindling mostly to murmurs, as she returned over and over to the comfort of the white flower. She had begun to think of it as her friend. When a voice would intrude—a rasping whisper in her ears—she would summon the image of the flower—its candle bud emerging from the earth, unfolding each of its four petals one by one.

When she appeared to be in her right mind again, Leonard, solicitous and still frightened, moved her to The El Encanto Hotel and Bungalows, a small resort in Santa Barbara, not far from the ocean. There, in the hotel's courtyard, surrounded by white adobe walls covered with purple bougainvillea, palm trees and terra cotta pots filled with geraniums, she discovered she was able to converse and conduct herself as a sane person. Though still on a modified "Rest Cure" regimen, she was permitted to receive mail and to write sane, dull letters to each of the children and to Leonard's mother.

> Dear Mamma Bacon—
> I must write to tell you and to show you how much better I am, and if I could have gotten hold of paper and pen and ink while I was in the the hospital, I would have written sooner. It is warm and clear and lovely here, so lovely that I can sit out of doors all day....[15.]

Patty Bacon was lying about the voices to Leonard and the staff at the convalescent hotel. She knew she must return to her family even as she felt the magnetic allure of the half-dream state. The image of the white flower sustained her, though the voices sometimes still surged and receded like waves within her mind. They often blended with the sound of the Pacific Ocean's waves breaking on the shore in the distance. Some part of her longed to stay with the voices and the story, lost forever to the "real" world. She fought these voices with every ounce of her strength, but she told no one.

Nobody knew except herself that she had no privacy of mind and thus no life within her mind. She resisted the intruders except for one unceasing female voice that emerged to hang on every thought. Patty Bacon could think, know and understand, mingle socially, but every motion of her mind was pain. In her sleep the voice did not leave her. Even reading was closed to her. She wondered if she could bear this secret for a lifetime. As she thought of this dire possibility, the female voice muttered, "peril, peril, peril, peril, peril" in her ear.

There seemed no escape, sleeping or waking, no rest—no end to it. Part of the hell of it was that she had to appear to others as if nothing about her seemed to be impaired. She wanted to tell someone. The world might say of her if it knew: "She has this one delusion but there is no harm in it," or it might put her in a safe place somewhere because the world must not be asked to believe that anybody ever really heard a "voice." She did not want to do either or did not dare to tell. Or not tell. Who would believe her if she did?

One night, very late, in the sanctuary of her small adobe bungalow, Patty Bacon leaned on the sill of her open window, breathing salt air from the restless ocean. She had risen from her bed, sleepless from the constant urging of the voice. She did not turn on the lamp, but a half-moon's pale light entered through the window to illuminate the room. The dim moonlight seeped over the dresser and mirror, the Mexican armoire, the bed, its sheets and blankets tossed like ghostly waves breaking over the floor. Her need to confess to someone about this voice had reached an unbearable point of intensity. In whose knowledge could she put her trust? "Run outside," urged the female voice, "pound on all the doors—go ahead—tell the whole hotel what's going on."

She clung to the windowsill, as if it were a slippery rock. Whom could she tell that she was crazy? That a voice was telling her she had no right to be herself—but who was she? She was Leonard's wife; she was the mother of Marnie, Helen and Alice, her three precious girls that one of the terrible voices had told her to kill. Who was this person in her head that wanted to destroy her life? And who was the someone else she could tell? She would have to tell herself.

And you hear the Voices, the Voices that you trusted because you heard them without understanding ... and let them in... and in and in and further in they went, to break the stillness in a hallowed place like owls that screech in the night. Listen to what we say, for we can Back It Up. And let us tell you—There are Limits. Do you think you are the solar system?

The hours that should have been yours; why had they weighed upon you so? Again and again... you had caught hold of time that shadowy keeper of your days; what then had happened to you? There really was something the matter with you then—yes, there was. The voices said "Yes, yes" with quiet cold triumph. "Don't you see?" the Voices said, "It can't be done." The Voices said, "Life is impossible." "If you do this you cannot do that. If you build here, you must crumble there... you poor child, you are a river, don't you know that? Like the mountain stream or the River of Life, you may twist and turn, but you cannot flow in two directions at once.

Then I will not be a river. I will be a light. Some lights are set upon a hill and some are hidden under bushels, but they stream out in all directions, they go every which way."…. Ah but we know!" say on and on those never-to-be silenced Voices. "Look at the past and the present and the people, and then come to our conclusions. We are the knowingness of centuries. Look at the unalterable—(The voices dare to breathe again the word "Law"). It

MSB, *Star Cluster Mandala*, 1936.

is the Way of Things.'"

Say it then. I am not the law. I am not the past and the present. I am not People. I am not the Way of Things. I am myself. [16]

Outside in the moonlight, palm trees threw spiky shadows over the tiled courtyard. She let go of the windowsill, pushing away from the edge as if she were falling back into water. She seemed to swim toward the door until she floated out into the warm Santa Barbara night. She felt the white cotton of her nightgown cool in the damp air against her skin. Large terra cotta tiles still held the previous day's heat under her bare feet as she crossed the courtyard. Except for a faint swish of breeze, all was silent and dark in the half-circle of bungalows.

Through the darkness she drifted, small and ghostly, toward a cluster of palm trees in the center of the courtyard where she lay down on the wide circle of earth surrounding their trunks. She breathed in the sea air and earth, felt hard clumps of dirt pricking through her thin nightgown. She lay still, wishing to feel her body as if she inhabited it, possessed it, sensed what touched her—not some other being.

When she opened her eyes to the sky, she saw the stars gathering into a vast wreath in a great arc. She knew it was a circle but could not see the whole of it because she was at the center of it. The sky was like an enormous black page, too big to see its boundaries, but she knew the huge curve went on until it came full circle within the rhythm of the process that created it. From the invisible point in space in which she seemed to be quite comfortably lying, she saw one star cluster as if it were the only one. It was in the shape of a heart very like one she had seen in a vision before in full daylight when she was in the depths of drowning in the tidal wave.

There was no escaping the heart-image—conventional as it seemed. She found it utterly beautiful.

MSB, *Celestial Swan*, Florence Series: 1928-32.

This constellation was a true cluster, three-dimensional, with its stars elaborately grouped as if in accord with some sublime mathematics, a breathing logic that had blown them into their places. The rich darkness was not absence of light but in itself a fullness of something that comforted the ache of the mind as the eyelid comforts the tiredness of the eye. Against it the stars shone with a liquid brilliance that was like light drowned in light.

The first cluster alone in the huge darkness was somewhat to her left and below her. The woman's voice, which never left and which was her alternating peace and torment through the delirium, was speaking to her now. It said: "That is only a tiny part. Now look!" Instantly then, the other constellation leaped into sight as if the thought like a genie had called them, and she saw an arc of the great circle, a chain of heart-shaped clusters like a gigantic necklace, curving high over her head until it was lost in the heights of the abyss.

In some way she knew—she was inventing perhaps—the scheme of this enormous galaxy. She knew it as if it were a cathedral that she had built herself. Each sun— or star—was a double sun having two bodies that were inter-penetrable, and their attendant planets were also double in this way, so that they had the same periods of light and darkness, dawn and sunset. Each cluster was formed in the exact image of the "Vision of the Heart," never fading on the horizon of each separate earth. Within each heart light there was an even brighter light, a sun within a sun, splintered by its own intensity into millions of jewels all clustered together and piercing each other by their rays, until in the center of all it passed the boundaries of light and became darkness.

Out under the galaxy of her vision she fell asleep, then woke to an ordinary night sky with a pale, ordinary half-moon and a few speckles of stars. Gazing up through the palm fronds at the moon, she began silently to tell her own story to her Self. It wasn't exactly a story but an ordering and naming of dissonant tones with lyrics full of questions and commands. "You," she began, in her own voice, "What are you trying to do—and What about *Her*?

She heard herself through to what she thought was the end of the story, but there was more. *You haven't dismissed the last voice*, said a voice—her own. Her dazed mind still clung to one distinguishable "person" in the voice. Still believing the voice was real in the sense of being "other" and beyond herself, she heard it as something, someone, "out there" forever. Since the dream of the deep well when it had seemed as if hope touched her with one finger and then withdrew it forever, this persona had been her guide—not kind, not beautiful, not prophetic; it remained the pitiless one that said, *Go back and suffer now and die if need be.*

She now understood, that she would go back to the world, to Leonard, the children, that life in rooms and houses and streets. The voice repeated: *Give up yourself, give up the one voice that brings relief from pain. This is your sacrifice.* That relief from pain had been the voice-image of her dream—the comforting friend. Now the last voice told her openly, without emotion—*You know that 'friend' was self-deception, it was only You.*

"You too," she said aloud, "were only me."

Then she saw and heard two streams of words—her own and the other's, both visible and audible above her head, one on the left, one on the right, saying and writing *You —and again emphatically, you you you you you....* They trickled downwards slanting inwards, coming towards each other, until exactly in front of her eyes, they met in one stream to form a Y, then dropped, tail first, into that deep well from which the flower had bloomed. With these words, the "other's" special task was ended; it had finished— ebbed to near silence. Now inconsequential like all the rest, the last voice merged with the din and nonsense that was pulsing in her brain. She was free.

The moon dissolved with the darkness as the darkness softened into a thick gray dawn. She heard the first birds begin to sing. Soon the hotel workers would cross the courtyard to start their morning chores. Patty Bacon rose from the ground, her thin body chilled, her nightgown crusted with dirt. She brushed herself off and for a moment stretched out her arms toward the moon fading into the light gray morning, before slipping silently back to her room.

As soon as I knew that my soul was alone in its sanctuary, I no longer feared the voice. I did not need to listen because the "other" was not listening to me. If I cared to, I could discern a whisper like a purling brook running under my conscious thoughts. It had nothing to say because it was nothing any more—only the discarded husk of riches that were now, I believed, within me.[17]

✳

The old clock on the landing announces the half-hour. It is 5:30. The fire has long since burned the last pages of the "case history" to fine ashes, leaving a faint smoky odor in the air. I imagine my grandmother making sure the coals are out before she returns to the chaise. Perhaps she thinks about closing her eyes for a spell while there is still time before everyone gets home. Time has always fascinated her. She thinks about how she once wrestled with it, how it tormented her. What did she not have time for? Her work, her art, herself. This was what precipitated the crisis, the "delirium" that she would eventually recognize as a mystical experience rather than a mental breakdown. She had written in an essay about time describing the frustration of trying to be an artist and a woman with a life and family. She had been trying to lead two lives, so desperate that she'd been shattered into splinters, that her own voice had become a chorus of "you" and "she" and "I" and "her." Somehow she had managed to write and paint about them all—-She/ I, You/Her—but there was more to discover, more to tell of the story. Patty Bacon resists the urge to lie back on the chaise and pull the afghan up to her chin. She must begin writing the story of the story:

> *Thirty years ago I wrote an account of a delirium—"A dream," I called it, but that was misleading, though I did not at the time mean it to be so. My description of it strongly suggests that the experience had lasted many years, a lifetime perhaps. The truth is that from beginning to end it lasted about two months. In 1922 I had undergone what in up to the minute slang might be called a "mental crack-up." I do not regret having recorded it, however inadequately, eight years after the event; but now, a lifetime later, some inner timepiece warns me of my need to bring it into clearer focus, if only for myself alone....*

She hears the clatter of the brass door latch, the voices of her two granddaughters and Marnie in the front hall. They will soon come in to the library to show her what they've charged at Kenyon's Department Store. Then it will be time to begin preparing for the cocktail hour and dinner, a transition from the day's duties to the evening rituals, old habits she cannot alter. She once dressed up in evening clothes and jewelry, when Leonard and all his relatives were still around to care. These social formalities are long gone. Nowadays, she simply goes to the tiny cell of a bedroom that was once a dressing room adjoining the master bedroom where her granddaughters now sleep. She will tidy up with a fresh blouse, a necklace, brush out her hair, re-wind and fasten the bun with the hairpins that have strayed during the day. She will change out of her sneakers, slip into low-heeled black shoes, and put on a little Tangee lipstick. She always wears the gold bracelet Leonard gave her with her name, "Martha," formed in gold letters within the band.

When we burst into the library, our arms full of packages, my grandmother looks up from her typing. My sister and I show her the underwear and pajamas, new sweaters, and wool skirts, school supplies. We do not ask MayMay what she has been doing, nor do we notice the faint odor of smoke from the ashes in the fireplace. We are used to seeing her here working at her papers.

✳

Over time the voices receded, though never completely. In later years, Patty Bacon confided only to her journal that one voice always lingered. She learned to understand the voice, the one that she recognized as her "self" and which she referred to as her "Friend in the Unconscious," also the title of her essay. Though it was my grandmother who was truly ill, ironically she never had the benefit of Jungian analysis. That would be my grandfather's realm and privilege a few years after his wife's breakdown. Vicariously, she absorbed all the Jungian lore she could from her silent, watchful position on the sidelines of my grandfather's life and became well versed in Jungian philosophy, which led to her understanding of the "tidal wave:"

> The word "integration" has, even within my memory, enlarged its meaning by taking to itself an extra dimension with nebulous boundaries as incandescent as the ring around the moon. (I wonder, is there a trickle of truth to that?) The familiar shadows of my forbears together with their first-hand accounts in letters, journals, and sermons, of the life-generating "conversion" are part of the selfsame thought. They are so near to me in time that I can allow myself, knowing that I do it, to look at an immense

panorama through the wrong end of a telescope. The panorama is the hurricane-swept landscape of the spirit across the world and down the centuries, and the image that I see is a sunlighted fragment encompassing about a hundred years, the years when for a not totally invisible minority the turnabout from the agonies of conversion the tortuosities of psycho-therapy had become an unavoidable something—to swear by, or at. To that minority the word integration seems more amenable, less superstitious than 'conversion' with its hell-fire associations. It seems to make all the difference that the more modern hells are scientifically vouched for.

Integration, as I understand it, has less finality than the rigid concept of a precise balance between highest heaven and most everlasting hell, and does not claim to be an unshakable or ever completed thing. I think it is like freedom. You have to keep working at it or you will backslide. We know of course that people did "fall from Grace" because they could not believe in their experience. Changing the words is not changing the thing at all. We should give thanks, especially now, today, that churchmen and psycho-therapists are working together, sharing and exploring a limitless terrain.

This is perhaps the time and place for me to say, most urgently, that I have never meant to advocate non-interference in a time of danger such as I have described; and if I have seemed to speak such wicked nonsense, forgive me, everybody. It has been in my thoughts that in almost any crisis, keeping one's feet even while losing one's head, is often the natural course of events. Help comes either from within or from without, or both.

It seems that both Leonard and Patty chose to disregard or avoid the "case histories" in personal accounts of their psychological struggles. They dismissed the advent of their troubles in similar language as if the melancholia and the "tidal wave" were "wild weather out of nowhere" as she put it or, as Leonard suggests, there was no excuse for such weakness when everything in his life was just fine. She literally burned her eighty-page account, while he chose to omit it in telling his story.

Leonard seems as well to have made use of his wife's experience with the "tidal wave." Here in the final poem of his collection *Animula Vagula*, written and published after his psychoanalysis, he subsumes her experience into his own:

POEM XXVII

There is dogwood in my soul.
The white four-petalled bract,
Pure, virginal, intact,
Gleams in the heart of the whole.
It has taken from the dark
That whiteness manifold.
Warmth trembles through the cold.
From lightlessness a spark
Kindles, and with the kindling
There is song in my ears
Formed by perpetual sphere,
That knows no dwindling.
Where the golden-rod and aster
And the sumach flamed,
I saw the Spring unnamed,
And at last am master
Of the pale lordly place,
To which my stricken eyes
Never dared rise
To look on that still face.
Beauty that is content,
The stellar fire
That the soul may not hire,
Nor the wit invent,
Have habitation with me,
Who passing by way of the Grave
Crossed over the sacred wave
Of the Spiritual Sea. [18]

Patty's luminous white dream flower, "the white four-petalled bract," appears in Leonard's poem as it appears in her paintings, an archetypal image, the "flower of integration," that is anyone's to use in poetry or spiritual reflection. My grandfather also borrowed her circle, a "perpetual sphere," to contain the dogwood, her waves, sea, stars ("stellar fire"), and gleaming heart, distilling the images of her visions into his poem in a kind of verbal mandala. I think it is the best poem in the book. The others tend to rant about the horrors endured by his soul lost in "Malebolge," or engaged in a war with death and darkness. As the poems in the collection progress, the tortured soul heals and becomes reconciled to suffering, death and life. Leonard's progress to "integration" was expedited by his time in Zurich, while Patty's journey remained solitary and sometimes perilous for the rest of her life.

I wonder what or if my grandmother thought about the use of her images in his poem. Did she feel as if something had been stolen from hers or was she resigned to seeing her words and visions published in her husband's poem without attribution? She was not alone in having her life experience and her written thoughts mined for material by a life partner. Zelda Fitzgerald and Dorothy Wordsworth, both of whom suffered severe emotional breakdowns and who both contributed much in the way of literary material to their male counterparts, come to mind.[19] *Animula Vagula* was published in 1926, soon after Leonard returned from Zurich. Consciousness of his wife's illness must still have been in his mind as he wrote his poem depicting the "dogwood in my soul," the same healing image she dreamed and painted.

III
Magic Circles:
Mandalas and Visions

*T*he *"case history" has now gone up in flames and what was chosen to be saved from the drowned rubbish-heap is in existence. Some of it is in the form of mandala paintings…. The mandalas are by no means remarkable as paintings, but still less are they "flights of fancy" or experiments. Two were actually visions experienced while awake during the delirium. A few years later I tried to paint them although I knew that it would be impossible to convey a fraction of their actual splendor.*

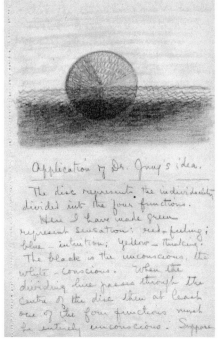

MSB, *Dr. Jung's Idea,* 1937.

As she slowly, covertly recovered, Patty Bacon began to paint the visions and dreams that appeared to her during her "tidal wave." She had no prior knowledge of mandalas, having discovered them accidentally when she painted a picture for a friend who described *the coalescence of disconnected elements of life coming together in symmetrical patterns—like a kaleidoscope. ...Then much to my surprise, I found that I had dozens of mandalas in my head. I painted only a few because I could not seem to find the time, or steal it; but it was great sport, it was enormous fun, although at times a little lonely, since it seemed impossible to explain that I was doing the opposite of what real painters do, that is—I was painting things, not pictures.*

Despite the restrictions of her domestic life and her self-criticism, she felt compelled to paint variations of beautiful circles filled with images, often with a white flower at the center. She discovered that this act of creation would eventually heal her fractured spirit. Later she would learn from Jung himself that she was painting mandalas. ...*I can still hear the voice of my friend as he explained and diagrammed the "sun-wheel"— magic circle—and the necessary openings in the protecting wall around the self—at least four gates to let in outside influences.*

✳

New York, March—1927.

A Checker Cab stops at the corner of 59th and Park Avenue at the entrance of the Anderson Art Galleries. A small woman in her mid-thirties dressed in a modest gray wool coat with a fur collar steps out into the chilled March air. The wind lifts the netting of her little hat's half-veil, and a tendril of hair escapes from the bun fastened at the back of her neck. Patty Bacon puts her gloved hand up to tuck the hair in and secure the hatpin. She scans the front of the building as if to get her bearings before stepping into the lobby. She has been here once before and knows how to find the stairs that will take her to "The Room" at the end of a corridor on the third floor. Still, she hesitates.

She is alone this time and unauthorized. Leonard doesn't know she's stealing this hour from her busy preparations for their trip to Zurich. Tomorrow she and Leonard sail for London on The Mauritania, then travel to Paris and Italy before going to Zurich. She must move quickly because she has not finished shopping or re-packing the trunks for the voyage. Their room at the Fairfax Hotel is chaotic, cluttered with things pulled out for this week before departure in New York. Leonard has gone out to meet with his banker to arrange money matters while they're gone. She is dreading being away from her three children for two whole months while Leonard continues his analysis with Dr. Jung—or, to be more exact, with Fraulein Toni Wolff. This will be his second two-month session. The first time he went alone. This time Patty is joining him at his insistence. The children will be staying in Peace Dale with their Hazard cousins.

During the days while Leonard is in analysis, she will paint—that is the plan, according to Leonard. She will have solitude and quiet in the hotel, and she will paint all the things that wander through her imagination that she never has time to finish or even start when she's at home.

She doesn't have much time this afternoon, but it will only be a few minutes, she tells herself. Afterward, she will walk over to Bloomingdales for two umbrellas and a pair of formal evening shoes she needs for the inevitable socializing once they're in Zurich. But first she will revisit Stieglitz's Intimate Gallery, "The Room," in the Anderson Galleries to revisit what she saw two days ago. She and her friend Celia had gone to the John Marin exhibition. She thought some of Marin's watercolors very beautiful, but some other paintings featured in the gallery had captured her attention, some large oils, quite disturbing to her, though decidedly interesting. Celia hated them, thought them gaudy, shocking, even obscene, but Patty has been unable to get them out of her mind. They are paintings by a woman artist, or, she should say, an artist who is a woman.

Patty feels anxious—about what? Getting caught? There is nothing wrong with going to an art gallery, but somehow she feels guilty. Yet she walks with resolve through the doors, climbs the stairs to the third floor, and makes her way to The Intimate Gallery. At three o'clock on a Wednesday afternoon, the small space is almost empty. Patty sees a woman all in black lingering near a reception table, the only furniture in the room, upon which a wooden stand cradles a crystal ball. As Patty passes by the table, the crystal ball goes opaque. The thought that it will turn clear once she's gone crosses her mind. She walks through the gallery where Marin's work is exhibited and finds what she is looking for in "The Room."

She lingers, staring at the somber grays and horizontal lines of the *Shell and Shingle Series VII*, but these, while intriguing, do not move her. It is the flowers that draw her: *Yellow Calla Lily*, *Dark Iris*, *White Pansy with Forget-Me-Nots*. Luminous, fleshy petals, pistils and stamens pulsing with some sensory memory she can't quite identify, yet she feels some stirrings of recognition.

Georgia O'Keefe, *Abstraction White Rose*, 1927.

One painting in particular pulls her in: *Abstraction White Rose*, a spiral cloud, densely white at a plush center. The spiral, shaded with gray and cobalt, opens outward with gaping dark hollows between the unraveling folds of the rose. Patty Bacon knows the dwelling place of this flower. She has been inside it and not so long ago. She remembers the vertigo of falling away from the center of herself—and from time to time the voice that still whispers:

You have been trying to live two lives. The good and the evil of it. It's good on the principle that two good things are better than one good thing—if you are sure you can work it out so that two plusses don't make a minus. If your this-life, on the one hand, seems to be satisfactory, and your that-life, on the other hand, seems to be getting somewhere also (measuring both by what they have to show for being lived) that's all very well—but a third thing has to be taken into consideration. That is the person who lives them both. What does it do to her? Does she round out? Or split in two? Or achieve a sort of combination of both? Suppose that she says to herself—"If only I wasn't trying to live my that-life. I would live my this-life much better." That is just what she does say, both backwards and frontwards, and then she thinks of the continued aggravation that means, like having one's hair pulled incessantly, and then of the strange fact that somewhere in the center of that heap of aggravation there is a joy that belongs not to either one side or the other, but to the struggle between them. There is the feeling that some day she will find the magic combination or press the magic button, or discover the magic formula that will bring the contradictions into harmony. Sometimes she feels very near to it, and sometimes aeons away…. She wishes she could

Georgia O'Keefe, *Jimson Weed*, 1932.

live a thousand years so as to go on playing it.

> *But ... How is it played? A great part of the time it is not played, just postponed. Sometimes with dull acceptance, sometimes with hope, sometimes with rebellion—always a split feeling. Is it time? Or strength? Or psychic energy? Or free energy? Or lack of talent? Or encouragement? What about time?—Talent? That question is unanswered except by the terrific kicking of the talent like something in the womb that is wild to get out. If it would stop kicking?—but it goes right on! Then energy. Where is it all? It never seems to be on tap... Is it buried under a mountain of fatigue? Is it the heart or the mind that is divided?* [20]

Some movement, a presence, brings her back to the Intimate Gallery. She does not know how much time has passed, but her feet are rooted to the floor. Then she is aware that the woman from the front desk stands silently behind her. She stares at Patty, dark brows arched over gray unblinking eyes, pale skin without the artifice of make-up, yet the face is a mask. Patty wonders how long the woman has been there, or how long she herself has been transfixed before the painting. She is flustered.

"I'm so s-sorry," she stutters. "I must have been standing in your way for such a long time. The painting is f-fascinating. Don't you think?"

The woman nods, but says nothing, a slight softening at the corners of her eyes. She looks to be about forty, austere in every aspect of her being—her black dress with its narrow white collar, her lean body, her demeanor. Patty begins to wonder in alarm if the woman thinks she is crazy, or that she might do something to damage the painting. She knows she looks harmless in her dowdy little gray coat, just an ordinary woman, someone's wife and mother. But then maybe the woman herself is crazy, maybe she recognizes what's underneath—the not so sane woman that Patty truly is.

Somehow those appraising eyes seem to know about her. But how could she know about the tidal wave? She begins to think the woman recognizes her from somewhere— The El Encanto Hotel? The dark eyes stare as if measuring her for something, and then in a low voice the woman says, "Yes, I like this one right now. Do you see what it is?" Patty does not know how to answer; she is not good at thinking of intelligent things to say to strangers.

She nods—and smiles, looking foolish, she knows.

"Oh yes, well, it is very late. I must be going." Now she sounds like the white rabbit.

The woman nods again slowly, a small smile. Or is it a smirk that creeps across her thin lips? Patty makes an abrupt escape from the somber figure, who stays, gazing into the white flower's shadowy spiral. She rushes past the reception table, just catching the reflection of a small woman in a veiled hat and grey coat in the crystal ball.

✳

I have gained some insight into my grandmother's circumscribed world by considering her contemporary, Georgia O'Keeffe. They could not have been more different as artists and as women, yet I've found several parallels in their lives and in their art. Until recently, like most people with an interest in modern art, I was familiar with O'Keeffe's work, its intense colors, simple lines, eroticism and magnification of objects, but I knew little of her life. I have since learned of her eccentricity, toughness, and independence, as well as what she faced as a "woman artist," a label she despised.

A few years ago, at a small exhibition of her work at the Shelburne Museum in Vermont, I stood before one of her white flower paintings, *Jimson Weed 1932*, in which the flower's white corolla is surrounded by a swirl of calyx and leaves in various shades of shimmering green. Though O'Keeffe strenuously resisted interpretations, I recognized something familiar as I stared into the bloom's center, where it darkened almost to black around pistils and stamens reaching out from the center. I began to see the mandala my grandmother gave me in 1965 for my benighted wedding. The painting, which she coincidentally completed in 1932, superimposed itself on the jimson flower. Though very different, even opposite, in form and style from O'Keefe's, my grandmother's white flower also gleams at the center of its concentric circles. I was reminded as I studied O'Keeffe's work that the flower represented the essence of Patty Bacon's life and spirit. The two artists shared this central image: the archetypal white flower as presented within or in conjunction with a circular shape or form. There is a story for both women that seems to want to tell itself through these images.

Like my grandmother, O'Keeffe suffered a severe nervous breakdown. She spent seven weeks in a hospital, and it took more than a year to regain her strength and emotional balance. During that time of recovery, she developed a close relationship with Jean Toomer, poet and novelist of the Harlem Renaissance. Though she was strongly drawn to him, she had learned through her ordeal that she could not expend her artistic energy in a romance. She wrote to him using metaphors of growth and fertility to explain:

My center does not come from my mind—it feels in me like a plot of warm moist well tilled earth with the sun shining hot on it …. It seems I would rather feel starkly empty than let any thing be planted that can not be tended to the fullest possibility of its growth…. I do know that the demands of my plot of earth are relentless if anything is to grow in it—worthy of its quality… If the past year or two or three has taught me anything it is that my plot of earth must be tended with absurd care—By myself first—and if second by someone else it must be with absolute trust …. It seems it would be very difficult for me to live if it were wrecked again just now. [21]

How similar this imagery is to that in my grandmother's dream of the white flower and her description of the rich earth from which it sprang. O'Keeffe's husband, the photographer Alfred Stieglitz, recognized her talent and enabled her success in the art world, but at the same time he forced her to make personal sacrifices so that her art would be served and take precedence over everything else. According to her biographer Laurie Lisle, and several other sources, O'Keefe had wanted children, but Stieglitz discouraged and redirected that desire into her art. Lisle states that he "loved her pure artistic spirit, which he thought of as 'whiteness,' and he didn't want it contaminated."[22]

MSB, *A Fairy,* illustration for a children's story, c. 1940s.

O'Keeffe's early painting, a white flower entitled *Abstraction, White Rose,* is womblike, a swirl of white tissue that spirals into or out from a center—like the wheel—a story but without a child. O'Keeffe came to think of her paintings as her children. When it came to splitting herself in two, she had faith in her artist self and made her choice. Though she remained devoted to Stieglitz, she ultimately had to liberate herself from him, eventually moving to her remote New Mexico ranch far from the art world, where she established her independence and freedom to live and grow as an artist.

O'Keeffe waged a constant battle with attitudes about "women artists," not only among her male contemporaries but in the culture itself:

> Even Stieglitz couldn't completely protect her from the wide-spread male conviction that being a woman was incompatible with being an artist. The year [O'Keeffe] had moved to the East, an art magazine published an article that declared that women can best create by giving birth. There never has been a great woman artist, the article explained, because it is impossible for a childless woman to feel as deeply or to see as clearly as a mother—and, of course, a woman painter with a child rarely has the time or concentration necessary for creating on canvas.[23]

My grandmother, unlike O'Keeffe, was fragile and unsure of herself as an artist; her work was illustrative, elaborate, decorative, narrative, delicate, often filled with androgynous human forms and faces. Certainly, my grandmother's style is not in synch with the artistic innovations of her time. She wrote of her disconnection to modern art:

> *.... I was not fooled by my own doodling. And that was not the only trouble. I was bothered by a current once more, a different one. For there was my flower, my jewel, and what connection did it have with something that I had been trying to decipher for a number of years? [T]he message of "modern painting," or of that infinitesimal part of it that is unmannered, that most pure painting that has no message because it is a message? It had no connection. I grieved a little and then I decided to the inevitable thing—that is—not paint pictures, but paint things.*[24]

The "things" Patty Bacon painted were mandalas and illustrations of her visions, filled like a kaleidoscope with minute and myriad delicate details, including human figures in symmetrical order. O'Keeffe's work is the opposite and virtually devoid of human figures, the imposing flowers and landscapes having no place or space available for humanity. My grandmother's white flower looks nothing like an O'Keeffe blossom;

it is neither large, bold, nor erotic. And yet, like O'Keeffe's white flowers, Patty Bacon's white flower draws the eye to a center of whiteness—the "pure artistic spirit" that both women strove to hold and sustain within themselves.

Distracted by duty and domesticity, Patty Bacon's attention was diffused through the needs of others. She was compelled to paint but had to steal time in order to do so. Only the family and a few friends knew of her work, while her inner demons almost destroyed her. Though she and O'Keeffe had to cope with the constrictions placed on them by a society that regarded females as incapable of becoming true artists, one woman prevailed, broke through the barriers and thrived, while the other remained hidden, her paintings tucked away in an attic room.

In *Modern Man in Search of a Soul*, Jung wrote:

> *The biographies of great artists make it abundantly clear that the creative urge is often so imperious that it battens on their humanity and yokes everything to the service of the work, even at the cost of health and ordinary human happiness. The unborn work in the psyche of the artist is a force of nature that achieves its end either with tyrannical might or with the subtle cunning of nature herself, quite regardless of the personal fate of the man who is its vehicle.*[25]

This describes Georgia O'Keeffe's and Patty Bacon's situation as artists and also as women, adding a significant layer to each sacrifice. Jung's statement assumes that the artist is male. As Jung suggests, an artist's struggles whether with internal or external forces can be extreme, but the reality of being female and an artist in the early twentieth century meant that one had to renounce one or the other part of the self. Each artist made her choice, and each experienced the pain of the sacrifice.

My grandmother would never be a professional artist, though for a time she wanted to show her work to an audience. Like her husband, however, she was rooted in the past at a time when the world was changing very rapidly and violently. Her mandalas and later her other paintings and illustrations were influenced by fairy tales and classic children's book illustrators N.C. Wyeth, Kay Neilson and Arthur Rackham as well as the work of Burne-Jones, Dante Gabriel Rosetti and other Pre-Raphaelite painters. She was especially inspired by William Blake's poems and engravings and fascinated by Lewis Carroll's Alice books. Coleridge's poem "Kubla Khan" was the inspiration for one of her mandalas. Patty Bacon's stylistic influences were rooted in Romanticism, as she was a true believer in fairies and other supernatural characters. She shared this inclination toward traditions from the past with her husband. Their art is antiquated and out of sync with the sensibilities and worldview of their contemporaries; in their work, however, one can readily perceive both the energy and, paradoxically, the fragility of two people who lived in a privileged world where the most important path in life was creating art and literature. It is a world that no longer exists—nor could it exist today.

✳

Dolder Grand Hotel—Zurich, 1927

Dearest Dear Children—

I am having such a quiet life here in Zurich that there really isn't <u>very</u> much to write about. We get up and have breakfast very late—sometimes in our room—It is nicer now than it was last week, for we have moved to a better room. Our other room had a lovely view, but it was very small, and I didn't have any room to paint or write, except my lap. The room we have now has just as nice a view, and we have a little sitting room besides a bedroom which is very cozy, and I don't have to sit around all the morning in a room where the beds aren't made—because, of course, if I made them myself which would be the really sensible thing to do, instead of waiting hours and hours for the maid to come, every one would be sure that I was crazy. That's the way things are in the world. Everyone thinks you're really crazy if you're not just as crazy as they are. You see I can't even speak German so as to tell a person that the reason I made the beds was because I wanted them made. And besides even if I could, that would be so simple that they couldn't understand it. .... So now I am going to tell you something nice—Two nice things in fact. Daddy has got tickets for our return trip on the Mauritania, which is the very fastest ship that there is.... Sometimes it seems as if I couldn't wait another minute, but must jump onto a ship and come flying home right now! The other nice thing is, that I have painted a lovely picture called "The Wave." ...It has five mermaids in it with green hair...[26]

On a sheet of hotel stationery, Patty Bacon writes to her three young daughters from her hotel room in the Dolder Grand Hotel in Zurich. On the front of the letter, a decorative block print announces the hotel's name, hovering over a very small, finely drawn picture of the hotel with its three minarets. Nestled at the base of a forested hill overlooking a village and the sea, the place looks like a castle in a fairy tale. The tiny script under the picture advertises "dernier comfort, Restaurant, plein air, immense Parc—6 Tennis, Golf links en face de Hotel... Garage...650 metres sur mer..10 minutes de la Gare."[27]

Patty and Leonard have been staying for several weeks in this fairy tale castle with all its luxurious trappings. They will remain in Zurich for about six weeks while Leonard completes his latest round of psychoanalytic sessions. These two months away from her children seem interminable to her. Life is quite entertaining for Leonard, however. Besides the therapy sessions, there are outings to Lake Maggiore, lectures, dinner parties, and nightly forays to clubs to hear jazz and dance. Leonard is out most days—and most evenings as well. He leaves for his therapeutic sessions first thing in the morning, often dressed for the tennis matches he plays after his hour with Toni Wolff. Then they all go off to lunch. Leonard has explained to her that analysis is incredibly painful, "like vivisection with no anesthetic." [28] He does not tell her what they talk about, but he assures her he feels more alive, more able to write than he has in years. The tennis and lunch afterwards revive and energize him.

Though she is usually included in the evening invitations, Patty does not have the energy to keep up with the pace of Jung and his female entourage. Dr. Jung surrounds himself with his "Valkyries,"[29] as he calls them, who are all in various stages of becoming psychoanalysts, like Miss Wolff, his constant companion. Their second week in Zurich they were invited out to dinner at a restaurant in Zurich with Dr. Jung and his wife Emma, along

MSB, *Nymph on a Wave,* possibly an illustration to a children's story, c. 1940s.

with a large group of followers. It happened to be Patty and Leonard's anniversary, May 16th, but she found it a rather strenuous evening. Emma Jung, in the psychological parlance that Patty is beginning learn, is a stoic introvert, in contrast to her husband's wild extroversion. Leonard describes Jung as "a most delightful combination of an Olympic athlete, Plato the broad-browed, refined scientist and dirt-farmer.[30] Jung certainly dominates a room, with his booming voice and large presence.

Miss Toni Wolff was not at the Kusnacht dinner party, to Patty's relief. Much as she has tried, she cannot find a way to talk to the dark-eyed, delicate beauty, who stands aloof and unsmiling whenever they meet. Perhaps, like herself, the woman is just shy, but she seems not at all interested to know her. In any case, Patty understands why Toni Wolff could not be there at the respectable dinner party with Emma. Dr. Jung's menage troubles Patty; she knows she is not sophisticated enough to feel at ease with the "arrangement." Even though Leonard has explained to her that Dr. Jung's "fragmented anima," a result of his difficulties with his mother, requires such relationships, Patty imagines that life in the Jung household cannot be restful. She wonders too at Leonard's newly acquired facility with psychoanalytic terms, and at Jung's confiding such personal matters to him.

During dinner there seemed no bounds to discussions of everyone's psyches—the divulging of grotesque dreams in the middle of the main course—a very rare roast beef. One woman exclaimed "Ah this boeuf! It reminds me of the large exposed buttocks of my dream last night. I was naked in the middle of Notre Dame!" A great roar of laughter convulsed the guests. Leonard pounded the table with his beer stein as Jung interpreted the dream for them.

Patty attempted a wan smile but remained silent. She felt her own substance slip away like water trickling down a drain. Dr. Jung had greeted her cordially but then seemed to forget she was there. She had successfully made herself invisible, hardly uttering a word all evening, but as they were leaving, he bowed and kissed her hand. It was after one o'clock, by the time the party broke up. Then it took forever to get out the door. In the cab on the way back to the hotel, Patty almost wept she was so exhausted.

She awoke the next morning feeling miserable about the children. She has been receiving little packets of their letters, ususally accompanied by drawings of princes and princesses, and a report of their latest activities from Miss Noo, their governess. Each packet brings with it more anxiety, but she writes cheerfully to ten-year-old Marnie about the previous evening:

"We had a lovely dinner party last night with the Jungs at a resaurant down town. It was a fine way to celebrate our anniversary. Dr. Jung is very jolly and funny and delightful, and Mrs. Jung is very sweet."

She told Marnie that she ordered dresses for each girl and about having tea with the Bayneses and Ximena, Mrs. Baynes's daughter. Patty closed her letter with, "Last night I woke up in the middle of the night and thought of you so hard, I though it must be just about your bedtime and perhaps you were thinking of me—Goodbye my own darling—From Mother."

Leonard, of course, is in his element here. That first dinner party set the pace for the duration of their stay in Zurich. Just last night, Leonard woke her up when he came in after four in the morning. She had somehow fallen asleep despite, as usual, being frantic with worry. He was drunk but in high spirits as he pulled off his clothes and dropped them around the room while trying to tell her about some hilarious comment he'd made in a rejoinder to one of Jung's hilarious comments. He flopped into bed, exhaling brandy and cigarette breath into her hair, clutching her in a clumsy embrace before he fell into an adenoidal sleep.

Patty lies awake until dawn when she rises quietly to move into the sitting room of their suite. In the gray light, she mixes the pigments, pale yellows and greens, shallow blues. She begins to paint the first of what she envisions as five mermaids with hair that floats around them like sea-foam spreading on the water. The curved line of the figure's slender body forms the front of a breaking wave. The arc of the mermaid's body ends in two small feet, instead of a fish tail. Patty concentrates so hard she is able to drown out Leonard's snorts and groans reverberating from the bedroom.

At eight o'clock she makes her way to the hotel dining room alone, sits at the elegant linen-covered table, eats a poached egg on toast, drinks orange juice and two cups of coffee with cream, just as she would at home. She takes a walk around the hotel grounds, and returns to the room to find Leonard up and preparing himself for his morning session with Fraulein Wolff. He kisses her as he dashes out.

"I must go, Darling. Miss Wolff will tell me again that I am infantile if I am late. I'll buy coffee and a pastry on the Bahnhofstrasse, and I'll be back to take you to lunch around one."

He bangs the door shut as he leaves, and a blessed silence pours into the room to bathe her like fresh water from a cool stream. In the bedroom, Leonard's stripped-off clothes from last night lie strewn on the floor. She picks up socks and garters, underwear, a used linen handkerchief. The bedcovers have escaped from the two pushed-together beds. Leonard, a turbulent sleeper, had kicked the pink satin coverlet onto the floor where it now lies in a peaked mound looking like a giant clam pried out of its shell. The sheets and pillows, free of their moorings, float on the lush blue carpet, whitecaps on restless waters.

Patty feels uneasy about the unmade beds. The sheets seem to flood the room, an inland sea foaming around her ankles. She remembers the wave, the tsunami that nearly took her away five years ago. She must make the beds. Should she make them? Perhaps it will inconvenience the maid. She must not inconvenience anyone. But the tide threatens to cut her off from the shore. She must make the beds. And she will write to the children, tell them of the trip home. She has been away so long—too long. Then she will paint the

Photo sent to Jung of a mandala, 1932. The painting is lost.

mermaid with green hair some more and call the painting "The Wave."

✳

Over the years, my grandfather continued his rather formal friendship with Jung, mostly based on his devotion to Jung and Jung's interest in my grandfather's literary scholarship and connections. Leonard traveled to Zurich several times, once on behalf of his cousin Rowland Hazard, an alcoholic who had relapsed. Leonard went to see what he could do to either get Rowland treated or persuade him to come home to Rhode Island.[31] Throughout the 1920s, '30s and into the '40s Leonard and Jung maintained a cordial correspondence in which they discussed a variety of issues related to

Photo sent to Jung in 1932 of a painting illustrating "The River Door." The painting is lost.

scholarly resources, translation and publication of Jung's writings. They also shared an interest in collecting pipes and Native American blankets. My grandfather often sent gifts for which he received thank-you notes from both Jung and Toni Wolff as well as requests for more pipes and blankets.

He was always happy to assist Jung in any way he could, whether it was as a translator, unofficial agent or literary advisor. It seems Jung felt free to offer an opinion on my grandfather's poetry. Leonard must have been somewhat dismayed by a letter thanking him for the present of his most recent book of poems:

"I have put my nose into it here and there, and I discovered palatable things. Please take this as a compliment. I usually hate verses. They are usually silly. But I came across some in your book that were not silly, they are even enjoyable. I hope that in the near future I shall be able to discover some more."[32]

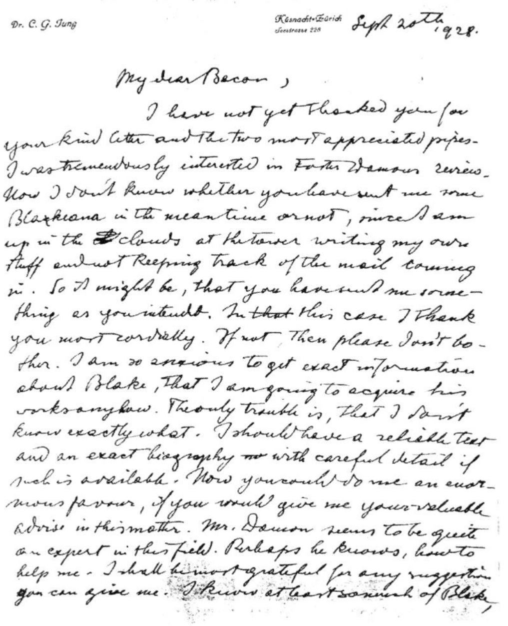

Dr. C. G. Jung — *Küsnacht-Zürich, Seestrasse 228* — Sept 20th, 1928.

[handwritten letter reproduced as image]

Letter to Leonard Bacon from C. G. Jung, September 20, 1928.

In spite of Jung's somewhat dismissive and entitled attitude, my grandfather was eager to please. He launched a passionate defense against James Hillyer, whose attack in *The Saturday Review* accused Jung of Nazi sympathies. The friendship was strong enough that Jung accepted an invitation to visit The Acorns in 1936 when he came to America to attend the Tercentenary Conference of Arts and Sciences at Harvard.

In 1928, Jung wrote regarding my grandfather's friend Foster Damon, a scholar and biographer of William Blake. Jung was very eager for information about Blake, as he had perceived a parallel with something he was working on:

> I shall be most grateful for any suggestions you can give me. I know at least so much of Blake, that I can deeply appreciate the truth of Damon's statements. The idea of the four Zoas is undoubtedly a most fundamental thought archetype. The earliest manifestation of it, known to me, seems to be [Pythagorean]. Please tell Mr. Damon, how much I was interested in his article. To know of this parallel with Blake is no small comfort to me. My unpublished so-called Red Book is exactly what you say of Blake's books: the text flows out of the pictures and the pictures back again into the text.[33]

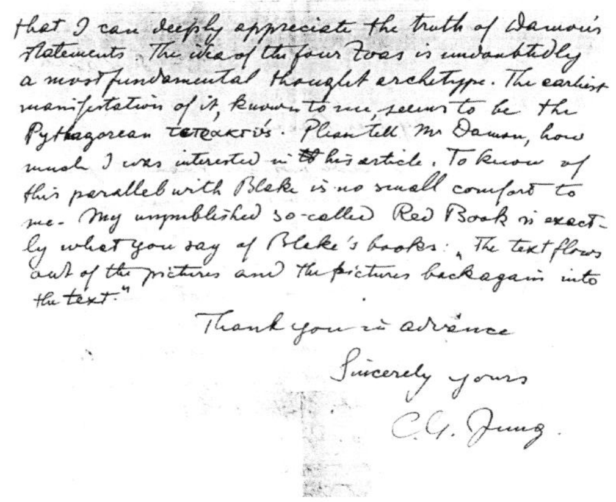

At the time of this letter, Jung was laboring over the text and illustrations of *The Red Book*, a manuscript in which he explored the unconscious mind after his falling out with Sigmund Freud. He spent sixteen years working on this exploration, writing his mythic stories in calligraphy and painting their characters and symbols. My grandmother was painting and writing her own version of a similar kind of story in an account and expression of her "psychological tidal wave." They even shared similar water imagery, flowing rivers and streams, to describe the overwhelming power of their experiences. Jung later would describe the time when he was working on *The Red Book* as one of the most important times in his life: "My entire life consisted in elaborating what had burst forth from the unconscious and flooded me like an enigmatic stream and threatened to break me."[34]

It must have taken great courage when in 1932 Patty Bacon sent Jung photographs of several of her paintings. By that time Jung had stopped working on his *Red Book*, but he might well have found these paintings and their haunting imagery relevant to his own work with mandalas and the inspiration behind them. He responded to her in a gracious letter I found buried in an old cardboard box stored in a shed at my Aunt Alice's house in Princeton.

MSB, *Radio Music Mandala*, c. 1930s.

Dear Mrs. Bacon,

I am most obliged to you for kindly sending me your beautiful Mandalas. Both pictures are really Mandalas, they are only different aspects of the same thing. Your art of drawing is really admirable. ...I shall be always grateful to you, if you are painting again something on the same lines, if you only send me a snapshot of it.

I don't know whether I ask too much, when I wish you would give me some particulars about these two pictures. You know, usually when one paints such things, there is always a sort of story or legend attached to it. I can't conceal the fact, that I should be interested to know it if it isn't too much to you to part with it. Even if those pictures shouldn't be associated with any particular kind of story, you surely have some ideas and impression or intuitions about them. It is not vain curiosity when I say that I am profoundly interested in the particular psychology of these pictures, in the contrary, because I find great value in them as well as profound meaning. ...[35]

Yours gratefully,

C.G. Jung

✳

She let quite a bit of time go by before she wrote him back. She didn't know where to start. Should she tell him about the voices? She began the letter rather formally and then launched into a long description of what had inspired the mandalas and what she wanted to create as a result of that inspiration. She might have written several attempts, since the letter in my possession is not a carbon copy and is unsigned.

My dear Dr. Jung

Although I have taken so long to answer your very kind letter, I hope you will believe that I have truly appreciated it and have thought about it a great deal. You have asked me to give you some particulars about these two pictures, some story or legend that might be connected with them, "if it isn't too much to me to part with it." On the contrary I often think it is too much to me not to part with it, although I have continued not to for a number of years.

There is no legend connected with the circular picture. She goes on to explain the story of her friend and Bacon relative, Kassy Hazard, who spoke about the inner sense of warring and disconnected elements in her life coming together in symmetrical imagery similar to a kaleidoscope.

I saw it instantly, and within a few days I made a little painting of it, which I gave to her—Several years later, while we were living in Florence, I made the larger and more elaborate painting of which you have the photograph. I did not know about mandalas in general at the time I made it, but I thought of it as something that had been developing slowly within a seed in all its complexity,

MSB, *Kubla Khan Mandala, 1936.*
Courtesy of Helen Drew.

and that suddenly burst forth with an outward streaming direction. Since then I have read and studied "The Secret of the Golden Flower" with the most intense interest.

That other picture is a rather large and colorful painting, and not what it appears to be in the photograph which was taken from a preliminary drawing—It is the first of a set of illustrations to a very definite story, which I wrote gropingly and with great effort because I had a strong feeling that there was a story somewhere in some lost darkness like a buried treasure at the bottom of the sea, and I very much wanted to find it. I wrote the story very badly—at least six years ago—a great deal of it was false and forced, but even now I keep finding more and more of the true bits of it scattered around at the bottom of the sea, and they all fit together strangely, each piece in its one and only place, until at last, after all these years, the thing begins to have a sort of symmetry, like a real mandala—very different from the lop-sided affair it was in the beginning—a sort of gibbous moon.

The letter goes on for twelve pages explaining the mandala as only one piece of a magnum opus, a long story she was working on that included music and dramatized scenes. She first titled it *Inlandia* and based it on her original "story" with the characters whose voices she heard in 1922: Hylas, Beatrix, Leo and Sophie. The title was an inversion of the title of the popular novel *Islandia* by family friend Austin Tappan Wright. His book was a Utopian fantasy, while her imaginary universe was a place she considered very real. Her story was an allegory; each character, setting and event stood for very specific human experiences. She expressed in the letter to Jung her frustration with the limitations of the story's text. She envisioned her book as a film with a musical score: "Now instead of writing, I am watching it; and I hear music. It is a movie, of course it is a movie. ... [The music] seems to be more in the shape of a sonata" with five movements.

That Patty Bacon heard music when she envisioned her book is not surprising. She was a musician, along with all the other creative, artistic things she could do. She played the piano and the violin, which was her favored instrument, and was part of a chamber music group that performed locally in Peace Dale. Every concert she went to in New York and Boston, all records she bought and radio broadcasts she heard, she wrote down in journals, with commentary on the quality of the performers and compositions.

I don't recall ever hearing her play her violin—her hands were too crippled by the time I was conscious of her love of playing music, but she still kept two violins and a viola on a high shelf of the "music closet" at one end of the living room in The Acorns. Sometimes she would let my sister and me take the instruments and the bows out of their cases, hold them, inhale the smell of the wood, settle our chins in the chin rest, pluck at the few remaining strings, rub old rosin cakes on the bowstrings, try to scrape out an impossible note.

Florence Series, 1928-32.

On winter Saturday afternoons she would stand over the heating grate in the living room, the heat slightly billowing her skirt, as she listened to an opera on WQXR, the old wooden cathedral radio turned up to fill the room with voices. She would stay there transfixed for the duration of the performance, even when we children were running in and out of the house. One of her smaller mandalas expresses her experience of listening to music: feathery circles of multiple wings—sound waves emanating from the face of a cathedral radio. On page twelve, her letter to Jung stops after the following paragraphs:

> These imaginings do not attempt to be suggestions. They are the result, I suppose, of reaching out to try to find a better form for this fantasy than I alone have been able to devise. No, I only partly believe that. I think I dreamed this movie principally for fun.
>
> But one way or another, I must be catching up with the belief that many must have had before me, that the moving picture now, is as natural and inevitable a medium for a poetic subject as the epic poem was a few thousand years ago—(and will be forever I hope). It happens to be the newest among innumerable musical and dramatic forms I have followed, but not superseded, the long poem down the centuries; so new that nobody has seen as yet what might be done with it. [And] times are too hard to find out. [36]

She did not send this version of her response to Jung's letter, but she did send something else. In 1956 she commented in her ongoing journal about the letter she sent him attempting to explain her paintings: *'Inlandia' is the story I should have sent. But although written at the time, it was in very poor shape. I answered his letter telling him a little about it, and sent him instead a copy of the record I had made of my psychological upheaval. He sent me a message by Kassy (Hazard), thanking me, but I have always felt that I made a mistake. I hope he burned the thing or lost it.*[37.] She had sent him the case history, the eighty-page manuscript she would herself burn in 1961, several months after Jung's death.

✳

New York, March, 1936.

Leonard and Patty spent the winter and spring of 1936 at The Plaza Hotel. Their eldest daughter Marnie had decided to forgo college and was studying acting and auditioning for Broadway plays. Helen and Alice were still in boarding school. The family spent a great deal of time socializing, to Patty's chagrin, as well as going to plays, films and galleries. She found time to paint while Leonard was busy with his clubs and speaking engagements. She was painting two new mandalas.

> *I have read Peer Gynt and Jung's Analysis of Zarathustra—Very Important. I have made one picture—One of the visions, a great black thing with star groups. I am struggling with something in the dark… and… beginning to think it is one of the pairs of opposites. I sometimes wonder if it is even Yang and Yin. I am not unhappy about it, so I don't believe it is a state of suspension—in other words a crucifixion.*

This piece was the vision she had of the dreamer in the star clusters. She was working on another piece at the same time that she called "The Temple Where the Streams Meet." *About half way through it I discovered that it had a great deal of connection with Kubla Khan. It is nearly done, and just now I am sick of the sight of it. Still I feel better for having done it in spite of my disappointment in it—a month from now I may not think it is as bad as I do at present.*

When the painting was finished after she labored on it all through the spring, she wrote of her relief in her journal and described a dream that followed. *My latest Mandala is done. It is a grand Mandala, but a bad painting. I was with Jung in a gallery full of enormous and beautiful jigsaw puzzles. Jung was having fun with the puzzles and invited me to join him. One of the puzzles seemed to be a sort of Medieval Madonna, heavy with gold and architectural effects, very mellow and old ... but the upper half was separated from the lower, and the sides and bottom were not exactly in place either. Jung told me it had not yet been put together. "But I see how it goes!" I said, looking at it. And I could see a sort of arched place with a little jog in the middle where the two parts were obviously all ready to be joined.*[38]

✳

Peace Dale, September, 1936

When Jung and his wife Emma came to The Acorns for a weekend in the fall of 1936, they were celebrated with a formal dinner party and an exhibition of my grandmother's paintings. Strangely, there is no description in my grandmother's journals of Jung's visit, an event I would assume to be momentous in her life. She who wrote so much about her thoughts and feelings would surely have recorded them. I have searched thoroughly among her papers, but with the exception of a few scraps of scratch paper with a number of hastily written quotes from Jung, there are no recorded details of the evening. She kept the paper scraps and would later re-copy the quotations into the back pages of a small notebook, which indicated to me that she tried to document something of what went on at the party. Acting as scribe, she captured snippets of things Jung said, most of which were his thoughts about Nazi Germany. There was one comment about one of the paintings included in the notes. In another notebook, the journal for 1936, on the back side of the very last page she had written: "1936—Jung's visit." The rest of the page is blank.

Many years later I asked my two aunts, who were around fifteen and seventeen at the time of Jung's visit, what they remembered of the party. Each had a very different memory of events. My Aunt Helen, the middle Bacon daughter, was a classics scholar, an ardent feminist who devoted her life to her work, and a very forceful character. She described Jung as being quite unpleasant. He was rude to his wife, talked too long and loudly and gave my grandmother's paintings scant attention. Her younger sister's perception was the exact opposite. Aunt Alice (Westlake), an art historian, married for fifty years and mother of four daughters, and no less a force, remembered the party as very exciting and Jung himself as gracious, kind, thorough and thoughtful in his comments about the paintings. She remembered he complimented her on her pretty dress. She also recalled that my grandfather was unusually quiet that night.

In attempting to balance these opposing "eyewitness" perspectives of Jung at The Acorns party, I have tried to recreate that night in my imagination, adding many invented details in the process. I don't know who was among the guests (neither of my two aunts could recall), but perhaps the Goodriches or the Peter Whitneys, devoted Jungians, traveled from Santa Barbara, California, to attend the Harvard Lectures and might well have been there. The Hazard family would have been well represented, perhaps to include the matriarch of the family, Miss Caroline Hazard, the Irving Peace Hazards, and possibly Rowland Hazard. Though I assume that my mother, Marnie, was also there, I was never able to ask her about it. She died in 1981 well before I began to research the story or even knew of the event. Neither of her sisters remembered her being there, nor did they remember each other's presence. Knowing my mother, I'm sure she would have had her particular perspective of the evening, so I have given her a presence in the scenes. In the telling, I have embedded Jung's comments verbatim in various imagined scenes as my grandmother recorded them on her little scraps of paper.

*

September, 1936

Patty Bacon sits outside the arc of a semi-circle of chairs as her guests listen with great attention to Jung. She writes quickly, catching his words on a few stray sheets of paper with a blunt pencil she's managed to find in the darkened room. Her only light is from the low blaze in the fireplace and the candles on Leonard's desk, a long library table stacked (neatly at present) with books and papers. The candles are burning down to their wicks and casting shadows across the expanse of the table's surface. The September night is cool, hence the fire, which flickers behind Jung as he stands before the fireplace. Jung's long shadow falls over his audience.

She can't quite believe she is watching and listening to Dr. Carl Jung in her own house and marvels that Leonard prevailed on the Jungs to stay the weekend with them at The Acorns. Jung has been in constant demand throughout his visit between the

Harvard Tercentenary Lectures and all the analysts and patients clamoring for his time and attention. Leonard's good-natured cajoling must have convinced Jung that a small party of devotees was just the thing to relax him after the tensions of the past few days. She likes to think her paintings were an attraction as well.

His acceptance was almost a last minute decision, so she has had to scramble to put a party together. Patty Bacon was determined to create a pleasant evening for the Jungs, inviting the guests, some of whom, like Leonard, had made the journey to Zurich for psychoanalysis. She had met Dr. Jung and his wife in 1927 the one time she

accompanied Leonard to Zurich, but she had spent most of her time in their room at the Dolder Grand Hotel painting mermaids with green hair while Leonard was in his sessions or playing tennis. The nightly dinner parties wore her out, so most of the time she stayed behind while Leonard joined the group. She was very relieved that Toni Wolff had not come on this trip. The relationship between Fraulein Wolff and Mrs. Jung is for obvious reasons strained, but Leonard adores Toni Wolff and keeps up a correspondence with her to this day.

Leonard drove the Jungs down from Providence where they had been staying with the Anglican Bishop. When they arrived, the men were in high spirits. Emma, pale and silent,

MSB, *Star Bridge Series, c. 1930s.*

waited patiently to greet her until Jung had finished exclaiming over the drive and the The Acorns. "Ah Mrs. Bacon, so delighted to see you again," he proclaimed in his charming Swiss accent.

Patty clasped Emma's hand, but before either woman could say a word, Jung broke in:

"Please forgive Emma for being so tiresome, she is always too tired."

Patty felt an almost indiscernible pressure in her palm and noted a bit of color suffusing Emma's pallor. She gave Emma's hand a secret, gentle return squeeze, and took her up to their room.

Leonard Bacon at the "Martha's Vineyard" fireplace, c. 1950.

I imagine Emma Jung following Patty, two silent wives of voluble extraverts, up the stairs in The Acorns, passing the grandfather clock on the landing, turning to the left directly to enter a large guest bedroom with a fireplace and its own bathroom. Remembering the tension of the handshake, Patty inquired if Emma needed anything. Would she like some tea brought upstairs?

"No, No—I thank you. I will not give you such trouble - but just a little quiet."

Emma hesitated for a moment, struggling a little with her English, then sighed: "They are so loud these men—talking all the time—these big egos—they do not even listen to one another. I am so tired with hearing them. I will stay here until he needs me again."

Patty could only nod in sympathy, thinking that perhaps Emma would lie down and rest, but Emma had already begun to open a large suitcase and was pulling out a pair of her husband's trousers to hang up. As Patty closed the bedroom door, she heard the deep wave of a sigh breaking and expending itself, filling the guest room with resignation. She remembered that Emma too was a psychoanalyst.

Throughout the afternoon and evening, Patty tended to the practical details of the dinner with the help of Holgate, their handyman, gardener, sometime chauffeur, and general life-saver, and Hilda, the temperamental cook. Patty is an incurable introvert, as she knows Dr. Jung would describe her, but over the years she has learned her duties as a hostess for Leonard, who revels in social life. He took great interest in tonight's menu, concerned that it should not be too exotic for the Swiss palate.

In the living room of The Acorns, cocktails and hors d'oeuvres were served in a blur of martinis, scotch and soda, bourbon. Patty could pick up snatches of conversation infused with Jungian lingo. Most of the guests surrounded Jung as he described the Harvard Tercentenary Lectures where he had recently been the honored guest lecturer:

> *A group of big brains assembled forming a big hydrocephalus—All the intelligences cancel each other, and the residue is an idiot.*

Was he saying the Harvard dignitaries were all idiots? The guests tittered appreciatively, though Leonard seemed rather subdued. Usually his laughter would be the loudest.

Soon they proceeded to the big dining room where they sat around the great oak table, all its leaves in place to form an elongated oval. Patty soon found herself in her customary state of anxiety, and was almost overcome by the sight of the glistening joint of roast veal. She nearly winced when Leonard sliced into its flank, allowing the juices to flow from its tender pink flesh. Libations of French wine flowed continuously in honor of their famous guest. Someone asked Jung what he thought about democracy.

He plunged into his interpretation with as much enthusiasm as he chewed his meat.

> *If a king rules badly you can kill him—but you cannot kill your democracy. What is he? an abstraction. He does not exist. If you have a democracy you are not governed. You put your affairs in the hands of and are at the mercy of a beast.*

"Democracy is a beast? How so?" Leonard questioned him.

Patty found herself hanging onto her chair, waiting for the brown sauce to swamp the gravy boats around the veal—a roast beast—surrounded on its enormous Limoges platter by new potatoes and a wreath of buttered string beans. She thought the table might capsize. The patter of silverware on china stopped. Everyone had been listening and eating at the same time, but now they waited for Jung's explanation. He raised his fork, a potato speared on its tines.

> *You see—Gold is the God of the Earth according to legend. He has been betrayed therefore you cannot buy him. When people put their gold in the banks they are worshiping the God because they trust him. They do not trust the government. What is it? It is just a wild beast. It is like putting yourself in the hands of a tiger. It behaves pretty well as long as the food supply is good, but when it is nothing but potatoes, then the tiger will get mad and eat you up.*

Jung growled like a tiger and bit with gusto into the potato. Everyone laughed heartily in approval. Patty was trying to remember exactly what he was saying, in the midst of her distress. Who was the god? Is it gold? And the government is a beast.

By the time the dessert arrived—pears swimming in chocolate sauce and vanilla ice cream served in red sandwich-glass dishes—the silver spoon in her hand weighed her down, as if to pull her into the cloying goop. The dinner seemed endless, yet she dreaded what was still to come. She could feel her bones floating in her dove-gray evening dress.

When dinner was over, the party made its way down the path behind The Acorns to "Martha's Vineyard," the studio cottage where brandy and paintings awaited the party. Leonard had built and named the Vineyard in honor of her, Martha, her formal self; it was supposed to be her "vineyard," a retreat where she could produce paintings and he could write. Patty preferred her small attic room in The Acorns where the light was better and she could be alone. She kept an easel and paints in The Vineyard's huge main room, miles opposite from Leonard's long worktable under the eight-foot window. For the purposes of this evening, however, the cavernous chamber provides plenty of space for a makeshift art gallery.

Then, what she had been anticipating with both dread and excitement began to unfold: the whole party gathered around her paintings arranged on easels set up at her studio end of the big room. Never had so many eyes gazed on her work at one time.

Holding after dinner brandies, the guests looked briefly at each piece, at the recurring images of rivers, and underwater boulders, of mountains and pale androgynous figures, luminous colors, the white flower image and star clusters. Somehow the paintings looked tepid and inadequate to her as she endured the inspection. At first, Jung and Leonard stood apart from the group while people murmured polite noises about the colors, the fineness of her hand, the minuteness of detail.

When Jung finally put down his empty brandy snifter, the guests stood back, their low conversations fading to silence as he moved deliberately from one painting to another. He peered so closely at one it seemed that he pressed his great nose against the surface as if to inhale its essence. It was the scarlet boy surrounded by flames floating above a placid sea, and below him, his opposite reflection, a cloaked female figure.

Emma Jung blurted with enthusiasm, "Ah yes—this is anima and animus. I have written much about this in a book...."

But when her husband frowned at her, she stopped mid-sentence.

Then Jung observed, *It is clear here that when the opposites are reconciled the center is lifted up to the surface of the sea.*

Stopping briefly at the largest painting, he announced: *The whirling vortex movement is trying to form a center for the ego.*

Then he pronounced a solemn verdict:

This mountain Mandala corresponds to the picture of the Eastern mountain with the sacred city on top—still in heaven. The palace has come down to earth. It is a substitute for mankind.

Was this true? He had seen more than she had intended, but it could be.

He gave her such a long look that she could not hold her own gaze. To her dismay, she felt a hot blush creeping up her neck and face.

✳

The inside of her head feels like the fragments of glass in a kaleidoscope waiting for another turn of the cylinder, commanding her to produce yet another vision—a wheel, a rose window, a clock, a spiral, a nebula—all spinning in her mind. She has waited so long for the time when Jung would see her paintings in reality, not just in black and white photographs. In this moment she cannot make sense of it all, but she does not have to think about it just yet. She was grateful when the talk about visual motifs in her paintings sputtered to an awkward though brief silence; Jung, eager to explain his thoughts about Germany, shifted the conversation to his interpretation of the swastika. She is happy to be the scribe, writing down his words with a blunt pencil on small scraps of paper.

From her seat outside the half-circle formed around Jung, Patty can feel the listeners' intensity. She cannot see their faces, only the backs of heads or their profiles. The fire flickers behind Jung who has begun to pace as he speaks. His shadow moves with him. Her gaze rests on Leonard, who remains uncharacteristically silent. She wonders what he's thinking about Jung and the "beast." Her three daughters sit among the group apart from one another in various states of ease.

Marnie, the eldest at nineteen, poses in a studied languor in an armchair near Jung. She's home after a season at the Barter Theater, showing off her British accent, newly acquired from the summer's acting lessons. Her wavy brown hair catches red glints in the firelight. She's been talkative and witty all evening about her summer acting roles. Patty knows that Marnie will have lots to say about the party. She'll be able to imitate the Jungs' accents for everyone's amusement after they've left.

MSB, *Daughter Helen and Her Father, Florence Series*, 1928-32.

Helen, her middle daughter, sits next to Emma and glares at Jung. She would have been better named Athena, this warrior daughter of hers, the most beautiful of the three. Her long, tawny hair is pulled back into a fat braid that reaches almost to her waist. Curls escape to frame her face giving her an aura of fragility that belies her ferociousness. She is angry with her father right now. They have been arguing about whether she should continue with school after she graduates. She is studying Latin and Greek in her first year at Bryn Mawr and wants to get a Ph.D. in classics. Leonard does not approve of women with Ph.D.s; in fact, he rudely told her that she had no use for one—"And Jung agrees with me," he announced as if that ended the discussion.

Jung seems to be on the defensive tonight, though he does sound sure of himself.

The Nazi symbol, the Swastika, goes anti-clockwise. This is an unfavorable direction according to the ancient eastern interpretation of the symbol. This is what I told them! Then one of these officials said, 'Ach! But if you are inside, it is going the right way.' 'Yes,' I said, 'If you are on the inside.'

Jung smiles—pauses. He raises his eyebrows at Helen—a slight nod to acknowledge her. He seems to want her approval. Patty can tell she is scowling, though she cannot see Helen's face fully from her vantage point.

The Nazi did not mention the subject again, Jung pronounces with finality, as if he had won a major battle. But he is not yet finished. Patty imagines Helen's skeptical expression.

The Nazis are trying to form a great mass of people into one, just one individual. Therefore there is no individual. What they are doing is what each man should do for himself inwardly. But it is being done to them from outside. Therefore the Nazi swastika is unfavorable... It is outside the individual. This is mystical. I did not go into all this with them—I would have got myself into an awful lot of hot water if they had understood it at all. They would have said, 'Oh, this is a religious attitude!'

Helen's shoulders are tensed, her back straight. Patty senses defiance in the wings and pleads silently to the heavens that Helen will remember her manners. At least Alice, is thoroughly captivated. Patty can tell that she is gazing wide-eyed up at Jung. She sits on the floor close to the hearth as he paces before the fire, her arms wrapped around her knees, gathered under the wide black velvet circle of her skirt. Jung charmed Alice when he bowed with a flourish and kissed her hand as they were introduced. She loves getting dressed up for a party, having chosen with great deliberation to wear her pearl necklace and a black velvet bow in her long, brown hair.

The voice drones on. Patty's eyes are heavy with fatigue, but she wants to catch Jung's words to write them down. She begins to drift off. How she longs for the night to be over. Another painting forms itself in her drowsy imagination. It is about the conflict between the two moods. There are two streams or two winds, or two rooms or two atmospheres....

MSB, *Tree Fairies, Small Series,* c. 1940s.

✳

Zurich, December, 1936.

Dr. Jung works at his desk tending to his correspondence. He is writing to Professor Heinrich Zimmer, who has recently reviewed his "Psychological Commentary on the Tibetan Book of the Dead" in quite a favorable light. Jung is pleased, so he is making an effort to thank Professor Zimmer and to write letters of introduction for him to several American friends. The professor and his wife, who is a Jew, are emigrating to America to escape the growing threat of the Nazi shadow. Jung is deeply disturbed at this thought, having found himself in the middle of a most unpleasant controversy that does not seem to dissipate. The business of Hitler—he has been accused of siding with Hitler, of being an anti-Semite. It is true he was fascinated, almost thrilled, five years ago by Hitler as the Wotan archetype that had overtaken the German people. And yes, he has his theories about the mental differences between Jews and non-Jews, but that does not mean he wishes them ill. Jung wonders at the persistence with which he has had to defend and explain himself.

Shrugging off the unpleasantness for now, he continues with his letter. He himself has recently returned from America, where in September he was presented at Harvard's Tercentenary Celebration with an honorary doctorate. It was a difficult trip. Supposedly, the psychology committee had preferred that Freud be their honoree, but he had declined, so they sent Jung the invitation. He had not liked being their second choice. And that bumbling neurosurgeon, Stanley Cobb, had introduced him after a windbag introduction to the filled amphitheater at Massachusetts General Hospital as "the esteemed Dr. Freud." Of course, Jung had made a faux pas himself. He and Emma had stayed at the Cobbs' house in Cambridge. Not realizing there were no servants, Jung had left his shoes outside the bedroom door to be shined. Apparently, Cobb had polished their shoes himself. No one said a word until he had overheard some embarrassing gossip.

MSB, *Tree Fairies, Small Series,*
c. 1940s.

Despite Cobb's gaffe, the lectures were naturally well received, and then there had been time to travel around New England. So far, he has suggested four friends for Professor Zimmer to contact, three at Harvard, one at Cornell. After the number five, Jung writes: "Don't omit to visit my friend Leonard Bacon, the American poet, whose most important work appears to be his *Animula Vagula....*" Bacon, he recalls had written that collection after his sessions in Zurich.

Jung sets down his fountain pen and stares out of his study window at the gray December morning, remembering the weekend he spent in Rhode Island with Leonard Bacon and his family. Now, there is an interesting constellation of complexes! Fragments of remembered images float across the proscenium arch of Dr. Jung's imagination, superimposing on the drab winter landscape outside the window. Leonard Bacon, a rich fellow, rather silly poet, quite the extrovert—he loves a commotion—and to be onstage spouting poetry. Big voice and presence.

The first time Bacon came to Zurich for analysis, Jung took him to a party and then out to Kusnacht where Leonard had danced all night with a German widow he'd picked up on the train from Rome.[39] Jung himself enjoyed such a party, to tell the truth of it. In spite of Bacon's egotism and need to be the center of attention, he was good company. At "The Acorns" (ridiculous name for such a large house), The Bacons put on quite a celebration with plenty of food, drink and the usual cadre of foolish Americans who hung on his every word. It was a pity he had to take Emma along on this trip; she always has such a stifling effect on his free expression. And Toni, left behind to tend the practice, was quite resentful and punished him, behaving like a reincarnated goddess and analyzing his motives ad nauseum.

When Leonard Bacon first came to Zurich back in 1925, Jung had passed him along to Toni. Men, especially American men, can be tedious patients, and Toni, though not so good with women, knows how to communicate with men. She has kept the correspondence going with Leonard now for over ten years; it is no wonder she was resentful at being left behind and replaced by Emma. But it would not do in America to have brought Toni. It is a sexually sick country—that combination of the Puritans and promiscuity—but so conventional too. Emma, "the good wife," had to be his companion on this trip. Since he had to quell the Nazi sympathizer murmurings all over Harvard, better the wife than the mistress who would cause even more talk.

At least Emma found someone to converse with in Leonard's wife, so timid, freeing up Jung to entertain the throng. Toni would not have given Patty the time of day. Ah yes, Patty, the wife. She is of the married/mother typology but an artist. Clearly there's an imbalance between the conscious and the unconscious—a woman artist and a sufferer—a deep introvert, something of the invalid. There is an internal oppression there. And of course she does not understand the necessity of masculine sexuality, always Emma's irritating neurosis.

Patty Bacon wrote him a letter in 1932 and sent photographs of her paintings. They were interesting, even beautiful mandalas. He agreed to look at them during their visit. She listened, writing down everything he said about the paintings. There wasn't much time to look at them as the other guests insisted on questioning him about everything. How he had to go on and on about complexes and psychoanalysis, politics and money, about the Nazis and their swastika. He had acquitted himself quite well, he was sure. He had been exerting himself to clarify his position, and this party provided the perfect venue. Patty Bacon wrote all those words down. He'd seen her sitting outside the circle, scribbling while he stood in front of the fireplace, the guests fanned out in the large living room like the radii of his aura. Had he written to thank her? He thinks so.

Jung picks up the pen again, re-reads his words to Zimmer, then adds a few more: "He lives in his private theater...." There is a faint knock on his door. "Yes," he barks. Emma enters with his mid-morning coffee. She sets the tray down, pours him a cup, adds the sugar and heavy cream, and stirs it, making sure not to let the spoon drip or clank against the teacup. She leaves as quietly as she arrives. Jung does not acknowledge her and returns to his thoughts.

He remembers that Bacon's three daughters were at the party. Complicated—a King Lear complex operating there. The eldest, Marnie, nineteen, an actress studying at a drama school, extrovert, leaning toward Eros hypertrophy; her type—something of the Hetaira mixed with the Amazon—fancies herself a poet too. She will move from man to man. Charming, verbally brilliant like her father—an irrational feeling type.

Then Helen, the middle daughter, the prettiest of the three—a Botticelli Aphrodite. Jung tenses. That name, "Helen," always causes a small, involuntary frisson, a reminder of his cousin Helene—that psychotic—who seduced him and duped him with her acting as the medium. She'd had him and his mother and sister convinced she was communing with the spirit world. Still, Emma had named one of their brood of girls Helen. But this Helen Bacon is truly an "animus hound." She studies Greek and Latin in school, insisted loudly at dinner that she would go to graduate school—an animus incubator—this bluestocking young woman of eighteen.

She'd watched him warily and glared at him when he had to interrupt the viewing of her mother's paintings. Then she would keep asking about Nazis. He saw Helen had been wearing trousers when he and Emma arrived at The Acorns that afternoon, though she dressed well enough for the party. No woman should wear trousers, an abomination that violates the feminine principle. She will never marry. Now, little Alice, the youngest, fourteen, sweet smile when he bowed and kissed her hand, so pretty in her black velvet frock. She might identify too much with her mother; she will marry and raise children properly, maybe amuse herself with studying art or helping her husband in his business.

Yes, it was for the most part a satisfactory visit with the Bacons. Jung resumes his letter to Professor Zimmer and finishes his sentence about Bacon's "private theater," The Acorns "…where it is all tremendously noisy and diverting," and moves on to item six.[40]

✳

Princeton, New Jersey—1996
Aunt Alice sits with me on the couch in her living room in Princeton. She looks the same as she always has, though she's 75 and her hair is snow white. Once a dark honey-colored brown, it is still pulled back into a prim bun tied around with a demure black velvet bow. We are excavating a large number of damp cardboard boxes full

MSB, *Small Series*, c. 1940s.

of mildewed papers, half-filled notebooks and binders with rusty rings and cracked black covers. These are my grandmother's letters, journals, and manuscripts of her essays and stories. Leaning against the Danish modern chairs are several portfolios filled with drawings and unframed watercolors.

These past few days, Alice has been her usual self, gracious and affectionate but at times remote and a little brusque. She is precise in her movements, at ease in the domain of her kitchen as she fixes meals, brings me cups of tea, prepares the inevitable pitcher of martinis that she and my Uncle John enjoy each evening before dinner. Intense and passionate in her adherence to what she believes in, Aunt Alice is a political liberal and a devout high church Episcopalian. As today is a Sunday, we went to church this morning—the first time in 30 years for me. It seems I can still remember the tune to "A Spacious Firmament on High" and sing the doxology by heart.

Since I arrived in Princeton from Ashland, Oregon, it has been raining—pouring—a tropical storm with extreme gusts of wind that whip the tall oaks and birches out in the back yard. Having lived out west for twenty-five years, I am not used to this kind of weather anymore, though I've never acclimated either to the scorching and desiccated summers of Southern Oregon. When the wind dies down, the trees in Aunt Alice's yard are so heavy with moisture they seem to cover the roof of the house, creating a cavernous effect inside. In this light, the sea-green carpet in the living room deepens by fathoms into the dark hardwood floor. On the back wall of the room, the storm's chiaroscuro light illuminates an early Renaissance painting of a Madonna from the studio of some obscure Florentine artist. Its heavy wood and gilt frame, inscribed in Latin—Ave Maria Gratia Plena—dominates the mild virgin within. My grandparents probably bought it when the family lived in Florence. My aunt, an art historian, has had this modest and possibly valuable virgin, restored since the painting, cracked and grimy, for as long as I can remember hung in the front hall of The Acorns. The only other adornment in the room besides the Danish furniture is a baby grand piano—also once in the parlor of The Acorns.

The painting, the piano and my church attendance of the morning have put me into a strange frame of mind. The room has taken on the hallowed atmosphere of a chapel where Aunt Alice presides as the mother superior. Familiar objects, the smell of my childhood emanating from the boxes, old hymns and rituals, Aunt Alice herself, are detached from the order of my chronological memory. I keep reminding myself that this living room is part of a suburban ranch house my Aunt and Uncle bought more than forty years ago; that The Acorns was sold almost thirty years ago; that I have lived in the west for twenty-five years; that I am 50 years old.

All afternoon as I read and sort through letters, journal entries and drawings, I question Aunt Alice and show her portraits of people to identify—people long dead from her past. Sometimes she jumps up from the couch and abruptly leaves the room. "Too hard for me to look at," she says in her terse way. She is the sister who chose to remove herself from the fray of the family dynamic to live a quiet, conventional life with her husband and four daughters three hundred miles from The Acorns. I think it is the smell that affects me most of all. The musty, slightly sweet odor of decay permeates the damp air. It is the smell of The Acorns, a house filled with books and papers, old wood floors and paneling, and plaster walls that never completely dried out in the coastal climate of Rhode Island, even in the winter. In summer, books, shoes and clothing bloomed with speckles of blue and green fur; beads of sweating salt coagulated in blue glass cellars, and doors swelled and scraped in their frames. The thick air of this east coast summer storm and the smell of my childhood home fill me with melancholy nostalgia.

For years I have wanted to explore the contents of the many boxes from The Acorns moldering in the storage shed next to the house. Up to now, Aunt Alice has always insisted that my grandmother's paintings and writings were of no importance or value, except perhaps as sentimental scribblings, of interest only to the family. The stories were just written for the children, the paintings the pastime of an amateur. In the past few years, I have gingerly approached her, trying to appeal to her sense of history; finally, this summer, inexplicably, she has allowed me to proceed with my research. In one box I find the 1932 letter from Jung to my grandmother about her paintings.

MSB, *Small Series*, c. 1940s.

It is a thrilling moment that immediately leads to my aunt telling the story of his visit to The Acorns, something I had not known about before. This discovery is my first inkling that something more than family research would result from this expedition. Alice was not aware of the letter's existence and, to my surprise, seems as excited as I am.

I find the thank-you note in the same mildewed cardboard carton as Jung's letter. This one is handwritten in blue ink, two pages folded in thirds, floating loose among the many other letters and notebooks in the box. There is no envelope to identify the return address or postmark. When I unfold the thin sheets of typing paper, I note with excitement the date: October 15th—about two weeks or so after the dinner party. A third of the first page is filled with a roughly drawn cartoon illustration just beneath the greeting: "Dear Mrs. Bacon." The drawing shows four characters seated at a round table, one of whom is the clear center of attention. He is the largest of the figures and appears to be speaking to three other little people. One seems to be female, the others of indeterminate gender. The three listeners have enormous rabbit ears, standing straight up in attendance to the speaker who has no ears (a suggestive, but probably unconscious, detail). In the middle of the table's circle the writer has drawn a large question mark. Next to the drawing is a caption written in an almost illegible scrawl: "I wish I could draw...And this [is what] I enjoyed so much!" My first excited assumption is that this letter is from Jung. The letter goes on to praise my grandmother in a complimentary but mysterious way:

> I am a great admirer of yours for breathing so much peace, so much light and saneness in this insane time, into your lovely home. And not only that, but, although you rarely speak and surely would never force anyone into this peace and light and great joy of Peace Dale—you are a very strong leader indeed in mastering such great weapons like patience, temperance and being always an example—so what else can one do but swim with the current of your forceful stream—and though this is one of the very best dictatorships one could wish for it nevertheless is a dictatorship.

I immediately begin to create an elaborate fantasy around the thank-you note that I will nourish for years. I imagine my grandmother sitting at the dining room table in the morning as Holgate brings the mail to her in the dining room at breakfast. She is drinking her second cup of coffee and notices the letter with a Zurich postmark. Her heart races as she opens the envelope. To her surprise and amusement, she finds a comical drawing at the top of the page.

I try to imagine what she must have thought and felt as she read the letter's text: "A dictatorship?" What an unusual way to describe her! She would never think of herself as having such power over others. The letter writer has understood her inability to speak out, her unwillingness to engage, as its direct opposite. Could that be right? Is this one of those paradoxes within her? Perhaps she can be persuasive at times. She will have to consider this pair of opposites. The image of her as powerful, of having a "current" in "a forceful stream," is something to ponder in light of her experience with tidal waves. The note concludes with a pleasantry:

> "It was a most perfect time I had and the rest did me ever so good. I am feeling it now having to work quite hard. Please remember me to Mr. Bacon whose wit, language and experience in his book I greatly enjoy—and thank you dear Mrs. Bacon so much for the time at The Acorns,"
> Yours—Illegible [40]

I think my grandmother might have found this polite and charming acknowledgment both pleasant and disappointing. There is no mention of the paintings. I envision her quietly folding the letter and slipping it into the pocket of her sweater. My imagination fails me after this. I leave the mysterious letter in a sweater pocket to make its way eventually to the damp cardboard box in Princeton, where I retrieve it and take it with me back to Oregon. There it would wait with the other artifacts acquired on that trip until I moved my worldly goods in another batch of cardboard boxes to Vermont to wait some more until I could begin to tell this story. Until very recently, I held onto the fantasy that the thank-you note had come from Jung. Even after scholars at The Jung Institute of New York did not identify the handwriting as Jung's, I clung to the possibility that Emma Jung might have written it.

Only after my Aunt's recent death, when my cousins sent me seven more boxes of archival materials I hadn't known about, did I discover the author of the letter. It was from a young German expatriate, Christiane Grautoff, a stage and film actress and close friend of my mother's from her New York acting days. Christiane was married to Ernst

Toller, a revolutionary German Jewish playwright and filmmaker who was expelled from Germany for his anti-Fascist activities and expressionist plays. He committed suicide in 1939. The Tollers had been occasional houseguests at The Acorns in the mid-thirties. Christiane remained friends with my mother and grandmother through the mid-1940s until she moved to Mexico with her daughter, Andrea. My mother and grandmother often sent her money and presents as well. Most of the letters she wrote are thank-you notes for gifts and hospitality.

My grandmother saved every letter she ever received from anyone, dating from as early as 1902 until 1967. The enormous volume of her correspondence depicted the busy, dramatic, intense, emotional world of the historical time—two world wars, the Depression, changing technology, the arts, social change, politics—as well as her personal world. Christmas cards, reams of thank-you notes, hundreds of letters from my mother and her sisters, from the time they were very small when my grandparents were traveling, or once-a-week letters when they were away at boarding school or college and over the years of their adult lives. There were letters begging for money or forgiveness from her sister Harriet, letters from former employees asking for references, letters of friendship from "Miss Noo" the children's beloved governess in Berkeley from 1923 when my grandmother was convalescing in the El Canto Hotel, until well into the 1960s. There were long missives from her California friends and family, and scores of letters from literary friends such as Laura and William Rose Benet, Richard Aldington, Mark Schorer; letters from the Sanskrit scholar Arthur Ryder, the Walpole scholar Wilmarth "Lefty" Lewis, the Blake scholar Foster Damon, and the comically named Bosworth scholar, Chauncy Brewster Tinker. There were many letters from Jungian friends like the Goodrich's and Whitneys—letters from my cousins, my brother and sister, and even a few from me, letters from friends in England, letters in French and Italian from their days in Florence, letters about illnesses, births and deaths, celebrations, accomplishments—thousands of letters. All of them told the stories of other people's lives, but every one of the notes and letters told some small sentence, paragraph or chapter of my grandmother's story, and they had in common a deep affection for her.

As I sorted and read fully or briefly skimmed through the deluge of letters, I was always searching for envelopes postmarked 1936 in the months after September, hoping to discover responses and reactions from people who had been to the Jung party. Though no more bread and butter notes surfaced, I did find among the massive jumble six more letters with Christiana Grautoff's (later Guterman) scrawling handwriting, one of them with the same cartoon characters seated around a large table. At first my disappointment was profound that I could not connect the letter in any way to Jung (except perhaps that Christiane had been among the dinner guests). Had he or Emma written it, how tidy and authentic that would have made the story of the party! Even though the less prestigious (however no less interesting) letter writer now has her true identity, the larger mystery remains unsolved: what really transpired that weekend the Jungs came for a visit? And what were my grandmother's true thoughts and feelings about it? Still, I have come to believe that the value of the message in Christiane's letter is more important than who wrote it, for she captured the essence of my grandmother's nature and what is was like to be in her presence. She did "breathe peace and light and saneness" into an insane world. And it was always so pleasant and easy to swim in "the current of her forceful stream."

IV
Center of Attention

Peace Dale, Rhode Island

December, 1940

Leonard Bacon at his desk in "Martha's Vineyard," c. 1950.

Leonard Bacon stands alone and morose on a December afternoon in the long room of Martha's Vineyard, his writing study. He gazes out of the large window near his desk. Extending from the high, beamed ceiling to a low sill, the window's twelve rectangular panes provide the room's only light, pale and drab, in the waning day. The distant acres at the far end of the room have disappeared into dimness and dust motes. My grandfather doesn't really see the gray sky or the cluster of chickadees on bare branches that, if he were in a happier state of mind, would catch his attention. It is two weeks before Christmas, but he is not thinking of the holidays

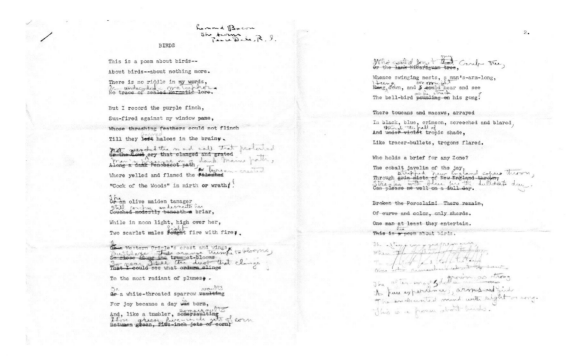

Leonard Bacon, *Birds* poem, written in 1953, sent 1953 Christmas card—his last.

as he stands by the enormous oak desk, a table more suited to a public library and a dozen scholars than one solitary poet. Assembled randomly on the table are piles of books, folders and portfolios rising in uneven stacks. A scratched Italian leather desk set with an ink-stained blotter adds to the geometric patterns on the table's surface. Random objects—a brass letter opener that looks like a dagger from ancient Persia, a pipe rack with an assorted bouquet of pipes, a cut glass lighter and heavy square glass ashtray filled with pipe ashes and cigarette butts—take up what's left of the space around the crown jewel of the desk. Front and center before Leonard's wooden swivel chair, a black Royal typewriter resides haughty as a queen mother. Within quick reach of the typewriter, a pair of binoculars for watching birds is jammed half into a leather case.

Writing is impossible today. Reading is out of the question, neither for work nor pleasure. Leonard has escaped to the study to collect his wits and his shattered nerves. More private than his library in The Acorns, "The Vineyard" works well as a refuge to separate him from the main house. Though only a short walk, the path winds off to a corner of the property hidden out of sight among old oaks and rhododendron hedges. It is his sanctuary, though he had intended to share the space with Patty.

I have often wondered why he didn't move down to the other end of the room so that my grandmother could have the light from that big window to work by. Perhaps it never occurred to him, and knowing her, she would not have asked him to make that sacrifice. It was in her nature and conditioning to defer to him. He loved birds, studied them, wrote poems about them; though the view from the window was quite ordinary—just the lawn at the south side of The Acorns, and some of the field below—he could see the birds from his desk.

As I imagine this particular afternoon in my grandfather's life, he sees nothing of the view from his window. He is consumed, outraged, in pain. Perhaps one hand still rests on the December 9th, 1940, edition of *The New Republic* where he has slammed it face down, breaking the binding. He has just read Randall Jarrell's lacerating review of his latest book, *Sunderland Capture and Other Poems*. Jarrell attacks three other poets, Witter Bynner, Frederic Prokosch and Ezra Pound. Not only did he pan all of their work, but the whole piece feels like a personal attack: "Mr. Bacon and Mr. Bynner are traditional in the sense that the appendix is traditional; they are the remains of something necessary under no longer existing conditions." Leonard feels the heat of his anger creeping up his neck again—bad for the blood pressure—his doctor has warned him. This damned "modernism" and whatever that term implies is an all out attack on the use of traditional form. It has infected the younger poets with hubris.

The poison goes on for six pages, but Leonard takes the first hit, feeling the burn of the acid words: Jarrell calls him the "licensed jester of the conservatives, a sort of muscleman of the *Saturday Review*.... Being in the age but not of it." He declares my grandfather and his fellow poets able to "write with impressive ease; their forms are strict, if awkward, their speech fluent, if unreflecting; how easily they triumph over the difficulties of which they are unaware!" Then the critic throws him a sop before the final caustic remark: "I have unkindly spent all my space talking about the limitations of Mr. Bacon's poetry; but inside these there are a good many rewards: vigor, arresting phrases, nice turns of wit, the reflections of an acute if conventional mind." For just a moment, my grandfather felt a little soothed—but then Jarrell finishes: "I should call his poems fairly good examples of a fairly bad sort of poetry."[41] Leonard muses: *A sterling example of damning with faint praise, layered thickly on top of that manure heap of damnation.*

Best not to dwell on this rack of humiliation. Still, his mind will not rest. He explained his "Defense of Poetry" to the world in the last chapter of the autobiography, clarifying his position that form is absolutely necessary to poetry.[42.] In spite of his discomfort with using the words "body" and "soul," with their odor of second-rate sanctity, he believes and has clearly stated over and over again, that like all things human, poetry has body and soul. It is clear that to Jarrell, formal poetry is an archaic and artificial form of expression. Of course, a great deal of poor stuff has been written in the old forms. And language that is merely metrical is horrible. But haven't they written still worse stuff in the new formlessness? And merely to have a yen for self-expression is meaningless unless it is allied with the succinct and compact. Measured rhythm is absolutely archetypal, as much a part of us as the disposition to eat meat is part of a tiger. Yes, the "body" of poetry is the actual words uttered in speech or printed on paper, and the soul is the spirit that informs the words, something felt by whoever is sensitive to such radiations. They must be in balance… these two …well. What's the use of such silent breast-beating?

Sadly, he is getting used to being called a pedant and a snob. Mr. Randall Jarrell is not the first to attack him for his loyalty to formal poetry, or even savage him personally. One critic accused him of being a Nazi sympathizer because he defended Jung against egregious attacks on his allegiances and his so-called anti-Semitism. Here, he, Leonard Bacon, is volunteering to work for the Military Intelligence Division of the United States Army. Right after Christmas, in fact, he and Patty will be staying in New York for the duration of the time it will take for him to prepare dictionaries in six languages for American Soldiers—French, Italian Spanish, Portuguese, Russian and German. The country isn't even at war now, though he can't see why we aren't helping the British more. At least he can do something useful instead of standing idle and wringing his hands.

Why should he bother with the critics? Was he allowing his complexes to come in, his anima to get mixed up with his feelings? This is what Toni Wolff would tell him. The venom of critics is innocuous and their praise just as unimportant. On the whole, he'd been gently used. Now and then he'd been panned—nobody likes that—but he'd had a tolerably good press, sold a few thousand books, even received letters from admirers. Not that he considered it fan mail, yet the letters were often pleasant enough to make him arch his back and purr, so to speak. He reminds himself that, after all, he has his induction into the American Academy of Arts and Letters on the 18th of

January to look forward to. It will be a grand evening and he'll be in fine company. The critics can go to hell.

No, he will not let Mr. Randall Jarrell upset him, ruin his Christmas, or even the rest of the day. Realizing it will soon be dark, my grandfather pulls his gold watch from his waistcoat pocket—4:30. They will just be finishing tea up at the house. No cocktails until 6:30. Damn! He'll have to find a way to fill the intervening time. He considers going up to entertain the ladies. Patty and the Hazard cousins' wives might still be planning their British orphan rescue and fundraising. Still feeling a bit bruised, he's not quite ready to play the congenial host for a crowd of middle-aged and elderly ladies even if he is related to most of them.

Perhaps a letter to Dr. Jung or Toni Wolff to tell them about the dictionaries. He switches on the desk lamp and sits down at the typewriter, scrolling in paper. He remembers Toni once saying in a letter that "Typing is a way to economize on libido."[43] He was always glad when she typed her letters, because her handwriting was impossible to read. He could use a little economizing of libido too, he supposed. But Toni and Jung are in Zurich. Getting mail to them is horribly slow, not to mention censored these days. Jung has warned him of this. For security reasons, he cannot mention the dictionaries, nor can he write about Jung's Wotan essay. A few years ago Leonard had offered to translate the essay for the American public. He'd even arranged publication with *The Saturday Review*. Jung's theory was that Hitler was an incarnation of the savage pagan deity returned from his hibernation in the German subconscious to wreak havoc on the world. What a mess that project had turned into.

After he'd sent his translation, Toni had written quite an insulting letter saying that Jung hated what he had done, that he'd robbed Jung's words of their life and spirit. She'd ended the letter with a swipe at *Rhyme and Punishment* ("…Your last book did not seem to me quite as good as the previous one.") because she didn't like that he'd written "An Analytical Dictionary" as a gentle satire of psychology.[44] The whole letter was a blow to his ego. He'd written back with quite a blast, accusing her of attacking not only himself personally but American scholarship in general. She had backed down, with apologies for unintentionally insulting him. Still, she'd wanted to blame him for the misunderstandings—he should have sent a letter along with the manuscript—but she had nonetheless reassured him that his "extrovert, negative anima" hadn't wounded her unduly.[45] It still rankled him to remember, and things had been somewhat cooler between them since then. He decides there's no point in writing to Jung or Toni. He'll write instead to his daughter Helen in graduate school at Berkeley.

Swiveling his chair away from the typewriter, Leonard picks up his fountain pen and a piece of onion-skin typing paper:

> Darling Helen,
> Your father has neglected you shamefully. But he has been leading
> a queer interrupted sort of life which perhaps explains.

He writes about his trips to Boston and New York, about Marnie and Philip's little cocktail party at their apartment, about being forced to go to see *Fantasia* with her mother, Marnie and Alice.

> Fascinating and incredibly bad. The Sixth Symphony with centaurs
> and centaurettes would just kill you—and the hippos in pink tutus,
> hideous. But the Pegasus family—white mother, black father and
> rainbow children all to the 'Pastorale.' The little black Pegasus was a
> delight in spite of the rest. But why Beethoven?

Putting the pen down, Leonard thinks how he hates going to movies and plays—except for Gilbert and Sullivan. He could tell Helen about going to *Iolanthe* too. He liked that a great deal, but really he does not enjoy sitting in a darkened theatre where actors on a stage or worse, a screen, pretending to be people in some real-life conflict are separated from him. He wants to be part of the play—in the midst of it so he can join the drama. This is his extroverted personality. Yes, he admits, it's his egotism (he knows what Jung would say). He likes being in the thick of action, not watching it in the dark. But he and Patty have made a small pact recently. When they settle in New York for the winter, she has agreed to make the rounds of social commitments, cocktail parties, receptions and so forth, with him and without complaint. In return, he will go to plays and films with her—when possible. Helen will like knowing that he was good enough to go to *Fantasia* with her mother and sisters, but he really didn't see why everyone in the world has been making such a fuss over a crass Walt Disney cartoon.

Leonard's watch dings. He tugs at the chain. He's made the time pass—it's six o'clock and dark outside. At last he can go back to the house to change for cocktails and dinner. Cocktails in half an hour; tonight he will fortify himself with a martini—or two. Alice is home from Wellesley for the weekend with a friend. There will, no doubt, be a young man or two as well, from Yale or Brown. Leonard always enjoys talking with them—holding their attention at the dinner table with his tales and recitations of poems. He likes to see if they know their Homer, Shakespeare, or Coleridge. And bless the poor boys, the threat of war hangs over them all. He'll get a sense of what these young fellows are hearing and thinking about that.

He encloses a check for Helen's train fare home for Christmas, and writes that he will be at Grand Central to meet her. This will have to be sent Special Delivery tomorrow, a Saturday. Signing the letter as he always does, "Your Loving Father, Leonard Bacon,"[46] he seals the envelope. Something accomplished despite this afternoon's upset! Determined to enjoy his evening, Randall Jarrell be damned, he knocks *The New Republic* into the wicker wastebasket by his desk and turns off the lamp.

I picture my grandfather, a big man, dressed as always in a suit, buttoning his heavy camel hair overcoat. He leans on a cane as he closes the door on the darkened Martha's Vineyard. Snow falls on his thick white hair and his broad shoulders as he makes his way up the short, dark path to The Acorns for cocktails and dinner.

✳

As the clock on the landing strikes six, Patty Bacon sits on the small cot in her dressing room that adjoins the master bedroom. She has finished combing out untidy wisps and pinning the thick rope of dark blond hair into a new twist at the back of her neck. Her evening ritual of changing out of her day clothes and dressing for cocktails and dinner is nearly complete. Except for the zipper of her dress, a new flowing, sea-foam green evening frock, recently purchased in New York, she is almost ready to go downstairs. She will need Leonard for help with the zipper and the clasp of the pearl necklace. The pearl earrings are clipped on; her gold bracelet is always on her wrist. Fortunately, dinner will be quite informal tonight, just Alice with her friends and Leonard. The meal will be something simple, roast chicken, not taxing for the cook, who has been ill and cranky with a cold the past few days.

Today has been another afternoon completely gone, another tea with Leonard's lady cousins and the wives of his men cousins. After the morning's chores and duties, she should have been painting or writing. She sighs aloud. The voice whispered to her all afternoon. While part of her knows that she is here to do one kind of thing—tea with the cousins' wives, meals, housekeeping—another part knows equally well that she is really here in this world for something quite different. She would not presume to call herself an artist, yet here, as ever, was this force that drove her to painting, drawing and writing. Why does she always feel as if she were two people opposed to one another? One is the sensible good person who knows that we are here on this earth and in this life, and that's just where we are and must live accordingly. But the other wants to obey the whisper that comes from inside. *That, of course, is what you are here for, that is what you promised not to forget. Then there is the mediator. It hasn't so far been able to decide whether it is better to give the whole field to first one and then the other, letting them alternate or to try and train them to pull along simultaneously.*

She has other ways of looking at her old dilemma:

> *Sometimes it is two rooms, but it is hard to pass from one to the other—the door is locked and I lose the key—or it is like the little door down the rabbit hole. I can't manage to be the right size at the right moment, to get through it.*
>
> *Sometimes it is the mind that drifts through the country that is itself, a country that is alternate stretches of desert and fertility—like the island of Hawaii—It is a lazy mind—it doesn't seek the fertile regions, it just wanders until it bumps into them unexpectedly. It perks up, takes notice for a little while, then just as inconsequently, drifts out into the desert again.*[47]

But, and here's the rub, she actually likes and enjoys the cousins and cousins' wives and what they are all planning to do, which is to open their homes to the children of several British families for the duration of the war in Europe. Until America decides to join the war, there must be something they can do to help. London, indeed all of England, has become extremely dangerous because of the German bombings, so a number of American families here in Peace Dale have been willing to work through their connections abroad and at home to get the English families safe passage to the States.

The purpose for the tea at The Acorns on this afternoon in December, 1940, was to plan a fund raiser and discuss where the British children would stay. Today's tea service was laid out in formal splendor—embroidered table cloth and napkins, silver tea pot and hot water ewer, china plates with little de-crusted ham and cucumber sandwich triangles, slices of orange cake, lump sugar, cream, and lemon wedges. The Hazard cousins' wives were in full form as well, being wealthy matrons in their forties and fifties. They all wore hats with veils or feathers and fur stoles—one swathed in a dead fox that, clipped together head to tail, chased itself around her large bosom.

They discussed dividing up the children among the Bacon and Hazard families. Patty is not so sure she wants to take on a young child now that her own are grown, Marnie newly married, Helen at Berkeley studying classics in graduate school, Alice in her last year at Wellesley. Except for Leonard's usual inability to stay still for long and the normal social obligations, things have almost quieted down enough for her to concentrate on her own work at last.

But of course the world and life are not so simple. Fortunately for her, the cousins' wives notice nothing of her reticence; they are used to her being a quiet mouse and launch into their plans as they eat cake and sip their tea. It is settled that there will be a benefit performance of some kind, a concert or play that will be put on during the summer. They cannot agree whether it should be a Shakespeare play or perhaps a gathering of local musicians. My grandmother thinks it a pity that Leonard did not come up from The Vineyard to help with some ideas for the performance. He would have known exactly what they should do. He was out of sorts about something this afternoon. Perhaps it's just as well he wasn't around.

As my grandmother dresses for dinner, I picture my grandfather heading up the porch steps toward the wide Dutch door, which has just been adorned this morning with a thick Christmas wreath. Admiring the scarlet velvet bow, he inhales the sweet balsam scent as he pushes on the latch. The door opens with its distinctive pneumatic whump, a sound my grandmother hears upstairs. She returns to the present, listening as Leonard enters the front hall. Instead of coming upstairs to change, he goes directly to the pantry about the drinks. He loves to mix the cocktails. There will be martinis tonight, and scotch or bourbon too if the young people prefer. She will have to deal with her pearls and zipper on her own.

✳

New York, January-May, 1941

During the winter and most of the spring of 1941, Leonard and Patty Bacon lived in a two-room suite in the San Carlos Hotel on East 50th between Park and Lexington. They had a tiny kitchenette with a hot plate and toaster where she could make tea and cook breakfast in the rooms, but they relied on the hotel for most of their domestic needs. Most nights they ate out at restaurants—Giovanni's, The Cosmopolitan Club,

The Commodore Hotel—often joined by friends or one or more of their daughters. While writing poetry and book reviews, Leonard crafted his dictionaries, making lists of words in all the different languages. A U.S. Army Major came several days a week to the hotel to confer about the work. They would become such good friends that the Major frequently joined them for dinner.

During this period in New York, Patty took the opportunity to read biographies, novels and poetry, to continue writing yet another draft of her long story, and to draw. Sometimes she tried to paint and practice the violin. She wrote a great deal in her journal. She also went to art galleries and concerts, listened to music on the radio, and

MSB, *Cartoon Series* (San Carlos Hotel). New York, 1941.

shopped. She went to the movies whenever she could, often by herself. Leonard was not interested in the movies. She was regularly occupied with her daughter, Marnie, a newlywed also living in New York with her husband, Philip (my future parents). They were practicing at being struggling artists. Having given up acting as a career, Marnie had taken up poetry and had recently published her first collection of poems. Philip wanted to be a painter and was taking classes at the Art Students League. They were constantly broke. My grandmother spent a great deal of time with the couple as well as a lot of money to prop them up financially. Many of her journal entries refer to buying dresses for Marnie, along with lunch, dinner, theater and movie tickets, and taxi rides for the couple. Helen, the middle daughter, was in graduate school in Berkeley that winter, but the youngest daughter Alice was in her senior year at Wellesley and often came to the city to visit.

The introvert and extrovert spent their New York winter dealing with blizzards and going to parties, many as honored guests after Leonard was inducted into the American Academy of Arts and Letters in January. Their social life was a constant round of cocktail and dinner parties, lunches and teas several times a week. Their circle of friends and acquaintances included many artists, poets, playwrights, journalists, painters, and sculptors. My grandfather was in his element; my grandmother was often quietly miserable.

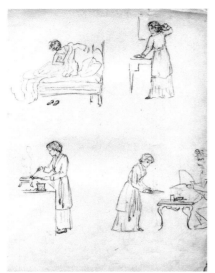

MSB, *Cartoon Series*
(San Carlos Hotel). New York,
1941.

She began a journal in January as soon as they moved into the San Carlos. She wrote in pencil on sheets of unlined, white paper that eventually accumulated to 204 pages, hole punched and set into a three-ring black binder. During their time in New York, the war was in full force in Europe, but there was still resistance in America, much to the distress of my grandparents, who had many friends in England and Italy. In spite of Leonard's moments of fame and glory and all the stimulating cultural activities of the city, the threat of war was a persistent theme in daily life, casting a pall over more personal, individual concerns.

Patty Bacon began her journal with a title page: "An Un-private Journal." I first discovered this tome in 1996 along with many of the paintings and drawings, her letter from Jung and all of her essays and stories. Decaying in an old box stored in the shed at my Aunt Alice's house in Princeton, her "Un-Private Journal" waited fifty-five years before anyone looked at it. When I saw the title, I realized then that she had written it with a reader in mind, whoever that might be—it turned out to be me. Into its pages she poured her thoughts and feelings about events, large and small, her many dreams, descriptions of people she met and knew, her marriage and children, the dizzying social life in New York, Leonard's triumphs, her own struggles. On the first page she wrote what looks like a poem that is a list, or a list that is a poem:

My mind is too full.
It is like a street in New York.
I cannot go forward in it.
I just look at what's there and stand still,

The agony of the whole world makes me feel repentant.
I carry that repentance
like a weighted darkness.

I have such a desire to understand and that desire is
                                    pierced

here and there by windows
of understanding.

I know,
and sometimes I want to tell
what I know.

I am not a Logos woman,
So perhaps
I never will experience the relief of telling what I know.

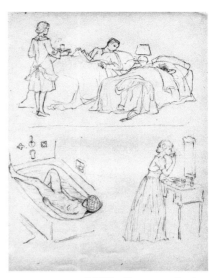

MSB, *Cartoon Series*
(San Carlos Hotel). New York,
1941.

There are many things I would like to write
and many ways I would like to write them.
I see them all, not vaguely,
but clearly.

"No room! No room!" whisper the Logosinians.

There is the everyday work.
Doing well, and yet keeping it in its place.
What about wisdom, sympathy, nonsense, rebellion?
Do they ever stay in their places?
Do they care about "a room of their own?"

Now for the list:

I want to write about marriage.
I want to write a diary that will be and yet not be a sort of stream of consciousness…
I want to write about the people who have taught me
and the people who have worked for me.
Sometimes I think I want to write short stories.
I wonder if my long story is dead,

or only sleeping?

I want to make color movies—of some of my original stories.

I want to make some writing and pictures that fit together the way architecture and sculpture does. I want to practice drawing and painting with a new technical approach.

I've always thrown away a lot, but I want to throw away more, and faster.

I want to try oils

I want to dash off cartoons

I want to draw "Alice" for the movies.

I want to paint The Rose Christmas Tree and The Red Bird and a lot more of my long story and some of the other stories.

I want to sketch places and people. I want to do some more Mandalas.

I have lots stored up and any number in bud.

I want to learn more about lettering

I want to make pictures of how I want The Acorns to be, and then I want to make it be that way.

I want to give up everything and do something to help win the war and something to help the English

Not just "my bit," but a lot.

I want to go to a good movie and forget about everything.

I want to go on living, and I want to be ready for death; even to choose it, in case —

I want to look like myself even when I'm old.

The list with its introductory lines was her declaration of intentions as the year in New York began, another ring in the concentric circles of Patty Bacon's swirling story. As ever, Leonard was the center of attention both in their outer world and in their domestic life, but somehow she would sooner or later accomplish almost all of the items on the list, with a few exceptions (she never made a movie nor did she paint in oils, as far as I know). Though their correspondence with Jung was curtailed by the war, his ideas continued to permeate their thoughts, especially Patty's as she questioned and pondered her life in New York. When she declared, "I am not a Logos woman," she was using Jung's term for the thinking type of woman, one who lived and functioned based on reason and the intellect. She had internalized Jung's theories about women's psyches.

It is no wonder she was of two minds, that two streams flowed in opposite directions, denying the power of her own intellect. The two voices within her spoke in opposition to one another, "the sensible, good person," and the "other one:" the artist, the selfish woman, whispering that she was on this earth for doing something other than being a good wife and mother, lived in her "Un-Private Journal." It was that "other" woman who consciously invited the reader to experience the divided world my grandmother lived in.

✳

While Leonard made his lists of words in many languages, Patty made her own lists: of daily chores and duties, of French terms used in English, and political paradoxes, of Native American tribes, pairs of opposites and "1000 little things." She wrote some of them in small notebooks, others on random scraps of paper and used envelopes, on the back sides of journal pages and the margins of books. She made an ongoing list of all the books she had ever read. She asked herself why make such a list, then answered her own question: *It's a game, a game of solitaire. I suspect myself of being too fond of playing solitaire. But ... in this one, when you finish it, you've got something. You've got the list and having had the fun of making it, you can now have the fun of playing with it, and there are endless ways of playing with it. ...* Then as an afterthought along the full length of the margin she wrote: *Also it is a protest against the superstition that because L[eonard] has read everything, therefore I haven't read anything—it is a kind of self-rescue. We need to keep digging ourselves out of the categories that people (with our own connivance) put us into.*

Her sense of inferiority is a motif that runs through all her writing, a wistful tune in a minor key. Sometimes she counters this painful feeling with resignation, sometimes with defiance. She does not begrudge Leonard his success—she celebrates it and him—but at times it seems there's never room for hers. Her mind is so full, "like a street in New York," and she is bursting to tell what she knows and understands. But she is "not a logos woman," not one who lives by the intellect, reason and structured thought. Or so she believes (with her own connivance) though she will chafe against the category, quietly struggling to keep her creative spirit alive—writing, painting, drawing, practicing her music.

＊

One of her earliest entries in the 1941 journal is the night of Leonard's induction into the Academy of Arts and Letters on January 18th.

> *Saturday evening Leonard was inducted into the American Academy of Arts and Letters. He (and all the other great ones, including Helen Keller) wore a purple and gold ribbon and sat on the platform, and Marnie and Philip and Helen and Alice and I, all dressed up in our best, best clothes, sat in a roseate row right in the middle of the parquet. Helen Keller was on the stage paying much closer attention than anyone else there. Edna St. Vincent Millay in a red dress and with flowing hair declaimed an ode. She trembled very much, but Walter Damrosch had a good time. He likes to talk; and Robert Sherwood made a very serious and good speech after being praised for ten minutes by John Erskine, which made him look as he stood there like a big, tall schoolboy who was very sorry and would never do it again. Robert Moses was given a medal that was reproduced on the wall in gigantic size for all to see by Paul Manship. Robert Moses made an amusing speech about all the reasons why he was such a good park commissioner, and now nobody who was there that night will ever make the mistake of thinking that it was easy. The Oratorio Society was on the stage all dressed in white and they sang music by Deems Taylor, Damsrosch, and Beethoven, accompanied by the NY Philharmonic. Afterwards we went to the Russian Tea Room next door to Carnegie Hall and had a bad time where we were stuffed into a smoky little room with a badly assorted company of interesting people sitting anywhere they happened to drop at a long L-shaped table.*

She soon tires of the glamorous evenings, but the pace is relentless, and dressing for them when she never seems to have the right clothing has become a dreary task. She hates shopping—it is boring, frustrating and expensive. The invitations pile up through January, February and March, three or four a week, including dinner parties at the sculptor Paul Manship's, and the painter Sheldon Pennoyer's, tea with Laura and William Benet, cocktails at painter Dorothy Jarelman's apartment, dinner at the

Colt's, where she met Peggy Bacon, lunch with Muriel Rukeyser, more cocktails at Mrs. Sidney Howard's—on and on.

She usually finds superficial conversation very difficult and cannot be comfortable or interested unless she feels some emotional connection to the person. It is hard when she meets new acquaintances to keep up her end.

> *What is known as "good conversation" is said to be stimulating to the mind, but the emotions are more important than is usually recognized. The things one hears said are often valuable but the excitement comes because they are said by somebody with whom you are in an emotional relation. Whenever the conversation is "mentally" very stimulating the emotions are stirred up. What I really hate about these parties is the falseness. You might catch someone's eye and acknowledge that this social dance is a farce—might through the mists of anguish even exchange a human smile. But most of the time—Oh those dead looks, those bored looks, the people give you at parties. They kill me and there's something so undignified about pretending you are having a perfectly delightful time, when you know you are having a horrid one and you know that the person knows that you know it.*

She admires Leonard's ability to charm people but does not know how to manage the crowds that he attracts. *Wonderful to think that I of all people should be intertwined with a man who so impulsively reaches out to people and captures them in the twinkling of an eye. He is a magnet, they fly to him from all directions, and more and more and more. The only problem is, when you have so many people and keep on having more, what to do with them all, when you've got them. I mean it always hurts me a little to get terribly cordial with people, and then drop it for months or forever*

Just as difficult for her are the political discussions going on at many of the parties. She tries to avoid them but sometimes finds herself stuck. At a party at the home of some attractive people named Laws, she found herself talking politics with three men while Leonard was talking psychoanalysis with the women.

> *Now and then a little remark was dropped which made me suspect that anti-Semitism and isolationism were in the air. Whenever we go to a*

plutocratic dinner party, and I have been to quite a number, it worries me horribly that the country is being divided. As it happened, nobody at the Laws wanted to start anything, but I think there was plenty of material on hand for explosions. Everybody was feeling desperately polite for some reason—Heavens—But it was a polite party! I think the Laws are not the kind that enjoy explosions.

It is true that people can believe wicked things without being wicked themselves—that's just a manner of speaking, because everybody is partly made of wickedness. The people who are fighting Aid to England, whatever reasons they may give—want the Nazis to win—there is no other possible answer.

In times of religious persecutions, people were punished for their "wicked" beliefs. No distinction was made between the person and the belief. Once it was wickedness and punishable not to believe in God in a particular way. Now it is wicked to believe in Nazi-ism, but we are making a distinction between the people that believe in it and the belief (not the Nazi's of course). I am running into more and more people in this country who are for it. It is incredible and it frightens me. Usually their way of putting it is to say they are down on the English—The English can't win and shouldn't win and it is wrong to help them. I would have more respect for their point of view if they would say what they really think—that they prefer Hitlerism and hope that it will prevail.

We are very apt to say, "He is a nice person, but he has awful beliefs" or "It is the person that matters, not the opinions that he holds—they don't count." In a time like this it is a dangerous leniency. "An overwhelming majority of our people favor aid to England, " say our journals. Is it true? I am beginning to wonder. If it is not true, we are no longer a country worth caring about.

✳

Waiting for Leonard to come home in the evening, Patty sits in the parlor of their suite, her journal on her lap and her feet tucked under her. She has been reading some Gertrude Stein and allowing herself to let loose on the page. She enjoys the freedom and the flow of the words as she leaves out periods and commas. She knows it's wicked of her, but she rather enjoys the thought that Leonard would be appalled if he read what she has just written. She is fraternizing with one of Leonard's literary enemies, an avant-garde poet, woman, heretic. She savors the guilty pleasure:

> *I think—maybe I am beginning to understand why Gertrude Stein doesn't punctuate and what she meant when she said writing has to go on and it's not because of the punctuation itself the little pauses for commas and periods etc. but because of the kind of writing that punctuation makes you do because after all we do not have our thoughts in one undulating line but in layers or perhaps I should say in something solid with a real shape like a house with a hall in the middle an entrance hall and rooms branching out in all directions one on this side and one on the other side and any number of them upstairs and a front porch and a basement and earth under the basement with worms burrowing round in it and a sun and moon and stars circling around above the roof and when you picture the house in your imagination all the doors are open to your imagination even if they are closed you can see right through them so their being closed doesn't make a bit of difference as long as you are just experiencing the house with your mind and that's what your thoughts are when you are really getting at them they are the house of your mind and the doors are all open in all directions and you can see up and down and right and left and in front and behind all at once and it's too much work to be always closing the doors that keep flying open as if there were a teasing wind blowing through the house every minute I know because I have been doing it for years and I think I will give it up because I don't care to work too hard on something I do for fun and I want to do it so much and then I can't do it because it is such hard work and I don't want to run away from it I want to run towards it and why should it be uphill all the way I hope you won't want to kill me when you get this Anyway*

> *I love you very much very much very*
> *Much much very*
> *Love much*

Love
Much much
And you
And love
And
And
Are you
You are
You are
Yes yes
You are
Yes you

This is me writing yes me it really really is
And I matter
It is not as I thought and as you
Thought I matter
Oh what is the matter? What is the matter?
You see you have helped me G.S.
And I thank you
Oh yes I thank you

Gertha Baconstein

＊

Patty has written down all the parties she's been to and is feeling a little better these days. Several weeks ago she thought she would die if she had to go to another party. But she kept right on going to parties and came through to a sort of second wind.

I must have been having a psychological rebellion. Every one I lived through was a sort of triumph, and that, I suppose was why I put them all down so carefully in my little black book. A triumph against doing something easy. It's easy for Leonard to go to parties and easy for me to go to a show. Therefore in our evenings together, when he is relaxing, I am working hard and vice versa. Well, we go to lot more parties than shows. So I am one up on him, or he is (one up on) me—depending on how you look at it.

We went to a reception for Robinson Jeffers two nights ago—and another cocktail party last night. I found myself facing both evenings with equanimity. I even had two dresses to choose between. But it turned out to be another ordeal.

At the reception there were too many people crowded into one small place. The noise was deafening. It made me hurt all over. There were people there whom I was thrilled to see, but conversation was impossible. Charlotte Kellogg, Lady Canby, Mrs. Saxton. The astonishing thing about that party was that it was in honor of Robinson Jeffers, and he is a famous recluse! And he is on a lecture tour!! He was standing up and taking it like a man, but he looked pretty miserable. There were a lot of sensitive souls there, and most of them suffering. I had a momentary glimpse of Edna St. Vincent Millay in a red dress sort of draped around a gentleman's collar (not that it was that kind of party). Then she disappeared.

She is fascinated by Millay—or "Vincent" as she calls herself. It was odd to see her trembling at the Arts and Letters ceremony, but she lived up to her reputation for unconventional behavior at the Jeffers reception. Millay has been so free in her life, open to experience and shocking, but fearless. Patty wonders about the rumor that "Vincent" was having an affair with Witter Bynner. It was wrong, she knew, but still she had to admire the courage it would take to live like that—and so beautiful in her red dress and flowing red hair.

Something funny happened when they were coming home from last night's cocktail party, luckily a small quiet one where everyone could sit down. She and Leonard shared a taxi with Mr. and Mrs. Clapp, their host and hostess of the reception for Robinson Jeffers the night before. *Apropos of last night, Mrs. Clapp said plaintively, "Vincent took Robin away from my party. She went to him and said, 'Isn't there somewhere where we can be alone?' Then they went into the study and she said, 'couldn't we shut the door?' So the door got shut. And Robin's party continued without Robin.* Patty wondered if the flame-haired Vincent and the shy "Robin" Jeffers escaped from the party together.

✳

Patty Bacon wants to do something for the war. She has tried to knit socks and a scarf with the recommended Red Cross wool, but the supply of wool is scarce. She begins sending monthly packages to a British prisoner of war in Germany through the auspices of the British Relief organization. Even though she feels this is not nearly enough, there is some satisfaction in going through the hoops for someone who has an identity and a possibility of receiving the benefit of her small efforts. "Stoker" Jones, as she calls him, was a stoker on a British warship before he was captured. She knows he comes from a poor family in rural England, wears a size nine shoe and has asked especially for barley sugar. Mailing the package comes with onerous regulations: the box must have no print on it and waterproof wrapping paper around the outside of the box. She hunts all over the city for waterproof paper without success and then decides to try oil-cloth. Triplicate copies of three different labels in three different languages must be made out to Stoker Jones at an alphabet soup address: OFLAG + STALAG XB—MARLAG pasted in very specific places on the box or the post office won't accept it. She must find a Notary Public to get the customs slip notarized. There is a weight limitation, so she purchases a small scale to use at home as she fills the box with tinned meat, orange juice, cheese, dried fruit, biscuits, hard chocolate, cigarettes, playing cards, soap, a pair of socks and a towel—and barley sugar.

When I present the first box to the post office window, I encounter resistance: "No you can't—the clerk begins in a truculent voice—then—"oh—prisoner of war." He approves of the oil cloth—hands me another tag. "Make it out like this one," giving me my own back to copy. I take it and copy it. Well, he didn't mean that, he meant something else and very crossly, "I told you lady... etc.—which was not true. I rewrote the tag, tied it to the package, while the clerk bully-ragged the next customer in the same tone he had used to me.

Patty Bacon sticks with "Stoker" Jones through the war and worries about him, worries that she isn't doing enough. There is more to be done, but what?[47] She listens to the radio avidly for news of the war's progress, bemoaning the isolationists and those who hide behind slogans of "America First" and "For America Only." She writes her fears and intentions on the backside of a journal page about shopping.

It isn't only the threat to our habits and institutions that makes us hate the thought of a Nazi victory although that is what we emphasize in most of our talk about it. It is largely that, but it is also our sense of outrage at the insufferable Nazi insolence. That we should be subdued by a nation whose institutions are anathema to us is direful; but that we should be dictated to by a gang of thugs who claim that they are a race of supermen ordained by God to take possession of the earth that their nationalism is the only nationalism destined to wipe out all others, their pride, the only pride, their way the only way, so coarse, so crude, so ignorant, that any accurate description of it would not be credible—for what could describe the haughtiness combined with swinish name calling the impudence that believes that the satisfaction of a few supermen is worth the heartbreak of every other man on earth, the ignorance that supposes that any "superior" man could bear his life on terms like that. The sordidness of an estimate of mankind so low that it envisages the whole world's population as forever cowed by a super-demonstration of brutality? That these people should ever dream of calling themselves our "Masters" and imagine that we would submit to it, the insult to every man, woman and child, to humanity itself, the outrage perpetrated by their words alone, to say nothing of their deeds,—it is that, that arouses the sort of fury that makes people say that they will die before they give in to it.

For myself, I will say—I will sacrifice. Heavens! What is sacrifice? We are all well acquainted with it. I could adapt myself to a new form of society, live in a tougher kind of world, work for my bread and butter (or bread minus butter) at drudging tasks, skim myself, even submit to regimentation, if it wasn't this regimentation. It is not these things that I fear. It is submission to something that I detest because it is ugly and low, and it is negation. Something that stands in the middle of my house, where it has come by stealth and trickery, stands amid the ruin of all that it could destroy by violence with its foot on the neck of my friend, its sword in the heart of my child and bawls at me to raise my hand and swear allegiance to it.

It is there—now. For myself again I say—not until the spirit is beaten out of the body by torture, and that could be done and might be, and would prove nothing; but not until then would I ever stop crying—"No, no, no, no, no!" to that.

It can make people say "Yes" with their mouths. Maybe everybody who is allowed to live will say "Yes" with his mouth. That is the kind of work it is laboring to make. And then—if it succeeds—it will have to talk to itself all the time for the rest of its life. Because, although there will still be lots of people, there will be nobody to talk to. Communication will be wiped out—Verboten

✳

In late February, Leonard is too exhausted to continue at the pace he's been keeping. His blood pressure is dangerously high and his thyroid is out of whack. He checks into the Presbyterian Hospital for a "rest cure." His doctor places him on a restricted diet—no fat, no sugar, no alcohol, no tobacco. Patty writes in her journal: *He is very tired after seven months of grinding drudgery at his dictionary work. That is a severe thing for an artist. It would be a strange thing if his tiredness and high blood pressure were*

MSB, *Leonard in his Element at the San Carlos Hotel*; New York Cartoon Series, 1941.

not partly due to a sort of spiritual rebellion. I think it probably is. I hope so. He <u>ought</u> to have a psychological upset after such a large war between conscience and disposition with conscience always on top. I'm going to tell him so.

Leonard's hospital room is on the 12th floor and has a view of La Guardia field (too distant to be exciting, however) and what's left of the World's Fair Exposition. It also looks out on Broadway and strings of green buses. All the 5th Avenue buses congregate there. He sits in bed surrounded by his books and papers or gets up and visits with a friend, Dudley Cates, on another floor. Patty goes to the medical center every day, a long distance on the bus—*so long that if you have to do it once you think you are killed, but if you have to do it every day it doesn't amount to much. Leonard is getting what he needs—first and foremost, a rest—a reducing diet which also brings down blood pressure; thyroid treatment for hypo-thyroidism, and visits from friends and lots of flowers. Today he had a stenographer and [got] through all his correspondence in one fell swoop. Leonard can make a hospital produce a stenographer. I can't make one produce a hot water bottle.*

The hospital seems to be a sort of hotel for the rest and rehabilitation of Leonard's famous friends and acquaintances. On the floor above Leonard's, Patty visits another friend, Kathleen Thomson. Kathleen is the wife of George Thomson, a British physicist, who won the Nobel Prize in 1937. He has been in America with his family to work on military uses of atomic energy and to get his wife and four children out of England during the Blitz. Kathleen is very ill with a mysterious condition that affects her adrenal glands, "some chemical deficiency." She has the same doctor as Leonard. Going to see her gives Patty a breather from the hours in Leonard's room where he is either holding court or complaining about the deprivations of his diet. She does not feel sorry for him.

I found Leonard in a welter of papers and letters and the mail I brought him added to the pile. Among other things he has a typewritten book of French poems by Yalta Menuhin. I picked up Whitman and read around in him while Leonard went through his mail. Leonard keeps telling me I look gloomy and troubled. He harps on it. I know what's the matter with him. It's his damned conscience. It's trying to tell him that I should be up there resting in a hospital and having nurses bring my breakfast, while he should be down in the maelstrom winning the war and beating Hitler with a dictionary. It's so easy to see through that he sees through it himself and

MSB, *Twentieth Century Alice*, c. 1940s.

yet he can't stop.

My persistence in taking buses instead of taxis doesn't help the conflict. I have an idea that I really can't afford taxis—at least not to 168th street and back every day. But also, I know that taxis are one of the ways in which I hate to spend money, except when going to the theatre or sending the children home on a cold night.

That night she stayed and had supper with Leonard at the hospital and came home on the good old Number 4. As the bus tore along, not stopping for blocks and blocks, she looked out the window at the river—gorgeous in the darkness of the winter night. The moon and lights from the Jersey shore glinted across the water, here and there lighting up chunks of ice and snow that bobbed around in the flow of the river. She considered going to a movie at the Translux. It didn't seem possible that there was no reason why she shouldn't go, but still her conscience tried its best to talk her out of it: It would be much too late when she got back to the hotel, she ought to write Aunt Caroline, or Marnie might call, etc. etc. She thought about an essay she wanted to write called "The Two Consciences." She had already sketched out an outline for it—like a wheel—a kind of miniature mandala. She liked to think of the conscience as "a Voice —of the two, one is an exhorting, the other a calling voice." It always seems to come down to voices she hears in her head.

But everything conspired against her conscience that night. *I stepped straight from the green bus to the red bus on 50th street and found myself at the movie theatre at exactly 8:00 o'clock with nobody needing me for anything. The movie was one of that crop about psychiatrists who get into a love tangle of their own—phony of course, but not stupidly done. I was glad I went to the movies.* I walked back to the hotel and went to bed with Canby's biography of Thoreau.

In the morning she woke with another attack of conscience: *Why don't I get to my painting? Is it because the surroundings are so poor—insufficient, light, space, etc. or is it really something else?*

> *Every morning when I wake up in my bed the prospect of getting out of it and washing and dressing and cooking breakfast and eating and clearing it up stretches before me interminably—a vista without end. I can't visualize enough energy to get me through it all. The fact that I know perfectly well that the whole thing will be completely done in a hour and a half or less, and is done every morning without fail doesn't convince me at all. But supposing that first hour and a half really was—a blank white page. Would any other hour of the day compare with it—be within miles of it? Why do I suspect it of being such a wonderful thing so nearly within my reach and yet fated always not to be?*

> *Here's the tension that those psychologists talk about: The desire to be a child again to turn backward toward freedom from responsibility. Opposite it there is conscience. It is and it isn't. That's a wholly negative interpretation. Conscience the enemy of creation as well as of backward timing, but they are opposites that have to come to terms (opposed to its opposite conscience). That must be really where the tension comes in. If*

> *there were just the negative desire to un-grow up there would be nothing to it—no meaning. Conscience doesn't come to terms with un-growing, it just conquers it. But create! "Ah there's another proposition!*

I always wonder about my grandmother's struggle to create. During that winter, she went to many art galleries and was surrounded by artists, many of them women, many of them friends. She was particularly close to Dorothy Joraleman, a portrait painter whom she had known growing up in Berkeley and felt a kinship with: *Sometimes I think she is a little like me which makes me sympathize with her.* She and Dorothy would go to galleries and art museums together. It was on one of these occasions that she saw Georgia O'Keeffe's work, perhaps for the second time.

> *Tuesday, February 4th 1941—Woke up with a severe headache and considered canceling my engagement to go and see pictures with Dorothy J. but decided not to postpone it for the 3rd time. ... So off we went, she tall and handsome in brown beaver, and I small and rather shabby in my old black coat. Anyhow the talk flowed ... We went to six galleries in the following order:*
>
> *The Matisse (odds and ends) among the two Picassos, one cubist and one what they call his monumental style. (I don't like it). One small gem-like Rouault.*
>
> *The Valentine—where we saw the Braque show—very beautiful, interesting— some Impressionists, delightful as always, particularly one Manet and one Sisley.*
>
> *Then we went to Stouffers for lunch—My hat blew off on 57th street, tore east for half a block and then shot out into the middle of the street. A man caught it for me. I never could have got it. I walked into Stouffers looking like the wrath of God. After lunch we saw an exhibition of delicious little paintings by Mager, then we went to the Georgia O'Keeffe show. Uneven. Not up to the others (?) Still I think she's an artist. (well, yes!).*

As she wrestled with her "conscience," and her internalization of Jung's designated "types," Patty Bacon somehow managed to create the art, to write the essays and stories over the years, yet she could never accept herself as an artist. I wonder too if she ever had any sense of her affinity with O'Keeffe's archetypal white flower. Certainly, given her sense of duty my grandmother would not have crossed the great divide into the life of an independent artist.

✳

On March 5th, 1941, Patty's birthday, Leonard came home from the hospital very depressed about his diet: no fat, no sugar, no starch, no alcohol, no smoking. He thought Dr. Bailey was really trying to starve him to death, yet he remembered to have orchids sent to their room for her birthday. *We went out for an early dinner, though Leonard could eat only a charmless meal of poached fish and steamed vegetables that nearly broke his heart. Back in the rooms for a long, quiet evening reading and listening to news broadcasts and music, Leonard was perfectly happy as soon as he got rid of his clothes. He sat in a chair in his red silk pajamas and blue robe and got livelier and livelier.*

There was a huge blizzard that same week, but Patty trudged through the snowstorm on her daily errands. *The snow crews are having to chop up the snow with pick-axes before they shove it down a hole. People are standing around in knots and watching. New Yorkers grumble at the storm and are thrilled by it. They all behave as if was the first blizzard that*

MSB, *Winter in the City*, Cartoon Series, New York, 1941.

ever happened in NY. Crossing streets—one foot on the Vent-du-Midi and the other on the Jungfrau—then splash! one galosh lands in Lake Leman and you leap over the Mont Blanc and a glacier or two to reach comparative safety on the sidewalk. It was snowing all the time too, but snow doesn't hurt like wind, on the contrary it soothes—I like it. I walked for over an hour.

She found it amusing that the spring fashions fought with the snowstorm for attention. *All the spring hats this year are like bunches of flowers—New York is like one big flowerbed filled with them; they line the shop windows and bob along the street. Nuts to the blizzard!*

Once he was out of the hospital, Leonard returned to his dictionaries and the Major, while Patty worked on writing her long story. Painting seemed to be eluding her and she stopped practicing her music. She packed up the monthly box for "Stoker Jones," went to the theater, read books, and wrote many letters to Helen and the family in Berkeley. Marnie and Philip were always in and out. She also went to visit Kathleen Thomson, in the hospital who did not seem to be improving.

Spring was slow to arrive. April was grim; they were plagued with bouts of flu, and deeply saddened by the death of the young daughter of some close friends. But finally things began to shift: *….in the middle of the afternoon a little spot of sunlight appeared on the rug! I felt like Robinson Crusoe discovering Man Friday's footprint on the sand.*

Leonard and Patty went to Washington D.C. for a weekend so that Leonard could meet with military officials about the dictionaries. She saw the Lincoln Memorial for the first time and went to the National Gallery. They also took the train to Peace Dale and spent a few days there to meet with The Acorns house staff to prepare for their return at the end of May. The kitchen was to be renovated and other repairs and improvements made to the house. Spring was in full bloom there and finally breaking in New York.

✳

May 5th starts as an ordinary day for Leonard Bacon. He writes letters in the morning and goes to the Yale Club to meet the Major to go over the Portuguese word lists, which takes a long time. His son-in-law, Philip, joins them for supper at Carlo's without Marnie, who is with a friend seeing an evening performance of *Arsenic and Old Lace*. It is good she is not with them this evening. Leonard has been hoping to have a private discussion with Philip about the couple's precarious finances — without Marnie there. She has a tendency to dissolve into tears at the mere mention of money, blaming herself with dramatic self-abasement and apologizing until there's no alternative but to write her yet another check.

Leonard intends to start the conversation by asking Philip how he and Marnie are managing to pay their rent. But first, he thinks, a little after-dinner brandy to ease into the moment. Now that he's almost at the end of the draconian diet, just one brandy tonight will help to fortify his resolve to be firm can't hurt. Philip already looks a bit wary. Patty is fiddling with the radio in an annoying way, looking for a concert they can listen to. Finally she settles on WQXR. The announcer mumbles something about the Pulitzer Prize winners. Leonard perks his ears up—he should listen—but he turns back to Philip, who is stuttering a bit about something, possibly to prevent the introduction of an unpleasant subject. He's just found a part-time job at *P.M. Magazine*. That's good news.

Abruptly, Patty shrieks, making him jump. He spills some precious drops of his brandy. "Leonard—you just won the Pulitzer Prize!"

"What!" He doesn't understand, can't understand.

She raises her voice and says again "YOU won the Pulitzer Prize—for *Sunderland Capture!*"

She says it again and again until it slowly begins to penetrate. But still, he can't believe it.

"I'm going to call *The Times*—this can't be true." He wanders around the telephone without doing anything to it. Philip beams on the couch possibly from relief or excitement, or both.

Leonard calls *The Times*, and they confirm that he, Leonard Bacon, has won the Pulitzer Prize for poetry along with Robert Sherwood in drama for *There Shall Be No Night;* Ola Elizabeth Winslow for a biography of Jonathan Edwards; Marcus Hanson in history for *The Atlantic Migration*. At last it has to be believed. *The Times* says so. There would be no fiction prize for 1941. Hemingway's *For Whom the Bell Tolls* was the Pulitzer Board's choice, but the President of Columbia University objected that the book was offensive, and the Board retracted the award.

Friends begin to call up to congratulate Leonard as he hits the ceiling, and so does a champagne cork—a bottle of champagne happens to be on hand. He thinks to himself: "Take that Randall Jarrell! You ass!" What a delicious irony that in this year of mean-spirited reviews, he, Leonard Bacon, has won The Pulitzer Prize for *Sunderland Capture*, the book Jarrell so cruelly panned!

Patty wrote in her journal the next day: *The roar and to-do doubled in volume after Leonard won the Pulitzer... Floods of telegrams and telephone messages—Leonard in seventh heaven. Two cocktail parties! First at Polly Howard's (wife of Sidney Howard— playwright), then the Sheldon Pennoyers. I shrank and shrank (I mean in size) the way I always do at cocktail parties. I undergo a terrible transformation like Alice after eating the wrong side of the mushroom—I feel my chin hitting my foot and it gives me a pain in the neck.*

✱

They would return to Peace Dale in June, which meant the return to large family gatherings and looming war concerns. The younger generation planned a theatrical project that raised money for British War Relief. The *Midsummer Night's Dream* production was a community effort performed outdoors on the lawn of "The Scallop Shell," which was Leonard's sister Susan's house. Hazard and Bacon cousins and friends directed, built sets, made costumes, acted, danced, sang and played music. Marnie played Hermia, Helen was Titania, Philip was Duke Theseus, and Alice designed and made all the Elizabethan costumes. Their friend, the lyricist, Bill Engvick staged and directed the play and played Puck as well. My grandmother played the violin as one of six musicians, according to the play program.

Patty Bacon got to do more than "her bit" for the war when it became clear that George Thomson's wife Kathleen was gravely ill (she died the day before Christmas, 1941). My grandparents took their youngest child, two-year-old Rose, into The Acorns and raised her until the war was over. Her older siblings stayed with other members of the Hazard clan, but Rose became my grandmother's child. The second half of the journal deals for the most part with the running of The Acorns and Rose's needs.

At the end of the year, Patty wrote a short list of events that made the year exceptional but which also darkened the horizon for the next several years: *Home in spring, Went through MSND (midsummer night's dream...), took on Rose, Marnie pregnant, Marnie, sick, Marnie better. We got into war. Kathleen died, George Thomson here, Christmas, War going badly, Singapore lost.*

✻

When my grandmother summed up the year 1941, she wrote: *There has been one perfect thing about this year: It has been Leonard's "coronation year."* Of her own accomplishments, she felt she had little to boast of:

> *Somebody asked me the other day what I had been doing all winter in New York and I couldn't think of anything. I might have said—I have written a book about what I have been doing all winter, it is on the window seat in my bedroom if anyone is interested, but it didn't occur to me.*

This characteristic self-deprecation seems almost pathological. I want to shout at the page. Late in the journal, Patty Bacon wrote a declaration of her brand of feminism. When I read the first three words of the opening sentence, I thought—here it is—she will take her stand. But I was disappointed as the sentence continued:

> *I am a feminist who is strongly inclined to the idea that Woman's Place is in the Home. Perhaps there would never have been a rebellion against that theory if it had not been accompanied by the belief, implied or expressed, that the tasks of the home were suited to their inferior abilities. Women's answer to that was to turn that work over to hired people whose abilities they considered really inferior, and free themselves for more "important matters."*
>
> *Taking care of children requires so much discipline and intelligence as any work there is, more than most. It is almost the most important work in the world and to do it badly is probably more harmful to our civilization than governing a country badly and running a war stupidly. Yet deep in our consciousness, deep deep under all expressed protestations is the belief that this, because it is the most disciplinary and the most confusing job in the world, should be turned over to stupid people so that intelligent ones may be freed for "social" works and duties. Almost all children are stupidly treated from infancy right through adolescence. If this were not so, how much would individual behavior be improved and how much would that improvement influence collective behavior?*

The revolt should have been not against being in the home, but against the implication that it was a job for inferiors. Not the division of labor, which is nature, but the assumption that one side of the division line is higher and the other lower—the reaction—tried to cross the line and put someone else on the lower side. The result is not invariably as expected. These "inferiors" are not necessarily inferior—quite the contrary. All people doing any responsible job should revolt against that, for every kind requires its own type of superiority. How childish are the people who believe that humiliation and indignity should be the accompaniment of certain kinds of jobs—jobs whose nature and whose difficulties they cannot know? And how much of the misery of the world is due to that childishness? [48]

She is right about the equal value of all types of work and the people who do that work, but my heart sinks every time I read that she sees that the "division of labor… is nature." She was a feminist in a way, but in such a confused and self-denying way. Because Patty Bacon so thoroughly internalized the Jungian designation of women's roles, she denigrated the possibilities within herself that could have led her to the lifework she so wanted to do. In my grandmother's acceptance of Jung's interpretation of the anima and animus, the male and female aspects within the psyche, she set herself up for the lifelong inner strife she endured. In a draft of an essay entitled "Sun in a Trap," written sometime in the 1930s, she explores what it meant to her to be a young girl and then a woman who always wanted more than anything in the world to be an artist.

As a child, she had believed that it was much better to be a girl than a boy and that she could do anything she wanted. She observed that boys couldn't be interested in anything but fighting, machinery, and sport, while girls could be interested in anything. *Music was ours, and make-believe, and variety and color, and sympathy and grace, and even nonsense, even seriousness. A boy wears armor almost from the beginning and will polish his shield forever if he can use it for a screen.* She would soon learn that being interested in something did not mean you could do anything you wished.

As she grew to adolescence, she realized she had been mistaken about her freedom: *I was more than ready to rush ahead and bruise myself against the cliff of a mental and inner life which I supposed was my own completely innocent invention. Naturally, I got*

MSB, *Animus and Anima*, c. 1932.

lost. I did not know what I was up against. …. For at that age, the boys, who in childhood had been misleadingly collective, were just beginning to discover in themselves, not rocks and cliffs, but continents of the mind, a treasure so immense, so awesomely promising, that they found themselves necessarily the seekers and guardians of mysteries, while the girls were now supposed to take their turn at camouflage and cultivate "mysteriousness" while letting the real mystery go hang—in case there was a mystery.

For a while she believed that women's suffrage would be the remedy for the injustices and misunderstandings about women's roles: *I believed in my ignorance of practically everything, that things had been gradually coming right for centuries and this gaining of the suffrage was the last and inevitable step. Probably now nothing more would have to be done for us.*

She was married and raising children, *doing what I had to do, what women do, and nothing but love was making me do it,* when she began to think that something was amiss. *I still persisted in thinking that I was happy, and for that reason I swam stubbornly against a deep undercurrent—which among other things was urging me to turn back to my past experience and unearth its meaning in relation to the present. ...Some day I was going to realize that my imagination had been thwarted and my sympathies imprisoned, first in childhood, by the protective coloring of boys, and later, in adolescence, by the unanimity of girls.*

She came to the realizations that there was a "law," that there were certain paths of creativity open for men only:

Yet customs and habits have been built around this "law" that are likely to persist even longer than our misunderstanding of it which is obviously related to man's passion for symmetry like a temple's; but Nature, in many of her life-patterns, decrees an illogical symmetry like a tree's, whose balance is fluid, not rigid, and not even visible, since it is partly underground.

Patty Bacon saw the tension between male symmetry and female asymmetry, *not as halves of one thing but rather like half an orange on one side and half an apple on the other,* and it was both cultural and political. She perceived the culture of Puritanism behind the notion that *the "arts"*

were unmanly, though unimportant enough for a girl to play around with if she wanted to. ... incredible, indefensible, unimaginable as it seems, [half the world] still believed that the men who were artists were trying to be girls (or something perhaps even worse), while the other half could not help suspecting that the girls who insisted on being artists, or indeed specialists in any field, were sometimes only trying to be men.

For one is related to a whole nation's—or indeed many nations' attitude toward the arts, and the other has to do with the relation of men and women to each other with respect to these arts and to everything else besides.

... I looked around me and saw what happened to women, and I looked inside of me away from my daylight self, and I had a strange sensation; for there he was. Inside of me was He. And I also knew that I would never be that he. Though really—I am.

I could and it would be wonderful, and it would be fun. It would be a relief to be that person—if I did not happen to be She instead. Yet, as things are, and as I must be loyal to my choice—or luck, it would not be easy, or even in the least possible, for she loves and is loved, but he lives in the dark and is unknown and unneeded. [49]

This was my grandmother's trap. She does not call her hidden "he" her animus, but that is what she believed was within her, her masculine being, "the artist," which she would have to renounce in order to do "what women do"—"what love makes them do."

My grandmother's two lives, her "this life" and her "that life," battled "with the terrific kicking of the talent like something in the womb that was wild to get out." To compound the problem, she was a woman seeking to integrate with the artist—the "he" who was trying so desperately to find his/her way out of the dark.

Psychotherapist Claire Douglas, who specializes in aspects of the feminine in analytical psychology, writes that Jung asserts "in his ...exposition of the anima and animus, man's feminine side continues to appear in a much more favorable light than woman's masculine. ..." Douglas cites Jung's description of the negative animus: "'Woman has no anima, no soul, but she has an animus... the astonishing assumptions and fantasies that women make about men come from the activity of the animus, who produces an inexhaustible supply of illogical arguments and false explanations.'" According to Douglas, Jung names a complex that bedevils many women; however, Jung's negative view of the animus goes too far and implicates a woman's very sense of her own value. Rather than ascribing the negative animus to a woman's individual and inevitable failing, it seems more fruitful to understand it as the baggage we all bring with us in a patriarchy: a consequence of the status and role of women in society, and of who defines us and what voices (Jung's included) we have internalized.[50]

Though my grandmother renounced what she believed was the "He" within her, she did not see him as negative. He was her positive animus, her creative spirit, her soul, the aspect of a self that Jung apparently thought women didn't have. While the anima was the essence of a man's soul to Jung, the animus in a woman, on the other hand, was what caused her to be difficult, contradictory and aggressive. My grandmother's conflict was complicated by paradox; when she declared she was "not a logos woman," she meant she was not rational, or oriented toward reason, something Jung disapproved of in women. Patty Bacon's mind had plenty of what might have been considered positive "masculine" attributes: she understood advanced mathematics, atomic physics, astronomy and studied the nature of time. All these disciplines require "logos" in order to comprehend them, but she either would not or could not recognize her abilities as either genuine or positive.

Denying one's own nature and abilities is an astonishing and twisted way to have to think about oneself. No wonder she was tormented.

.... I was bothered by a current once more....It would be too easy to say now, that because I turned my back on the thought of going a man's way, (I don't like calling it that), but whatever I am talking about, it might have reshaped my inadequate tools, I found instead these flowers of life which belong to a woman's (?) the way long known to be synonymous with darkness. Too easy to say because it is almost true. It seemed to be true, that I was able to have this experience for the very reason that I had not a man's, but a woman's opportunity. But since, thank God, it is not true, and the florescence cannot in any sense be thought of as compensation for being a human being, male or female, shall I call "it" compensation when I know that it is a pact with the Spirit of Life, and a rendez-vous with Death—this playful thing.

My grandmother placed a note in the text of "Sun in a Trap" to end the essay at this point. She crossed out the final paragraph. "The flowers of life" and the "playful thing" she refers to is the mandala. Creating "things" which she would not call art helped her to heal, but she replayed and retold the story as a work of art at every painful turn of the wheel:

It may be that women could contribute more from this side of life than men, for the reason that many, probably a majority of women, think this dark way and do not think the other, at least not very well. I know, or rather, I do not really know, how old this idea is. Woman is dark and Man is radiant bright. Eros and Logos, Yin and Yang. It is so old that who can know how many names it has?

At any rate it seems to be less unendurable for women to bear the burden of much knowledge that they cannot impart, than for men, for whom the necessity to give what has been given, is absolute. But for either man or woman it is anguish to bring what was dark up into the light, and for both it is possible.

She was the most kind and loving mother and grandmother and yet she passed the legacy of a divided self along to her daughters and granddaughters. My mother and her two sisters followed three very different paths in their personal lives. They all achieved success of varying degrees as women working in the world, yet the balancing act inherent in the personal choices they made was a always a struggle. My mother, Marnie, a novelist and poet lived a life of constant emotional and financial instability; she always wrote and worked as writer, but she was restless and perpetually self-deluded in her romantic life. She married three times, each husband more disastrous than the last. Helen, a highly respected classics scholar, believed that if she wanted to sustain her academic career she couldn't marry or have a family; she chose to live alone but suffered all her life from various physical illnesses and several serious emotional breakdowns. Alice, the most resilient and stable of the three Bacon sisters, chose the conventional path of husband and family over her career as an art historian. Balancing a professional life with her domestic life was not an option, so it was sacrificed until she could find ways to integrate her training and experience into her life after her children grew up. I too have experienced the two voices, the two directions, and often made the wrong choice or delayed making one so that my inaction made the choice for me. Sometimes that worked out.

I find myself having to make a list of the emotions and thoughts that occur as I read my grandmother's journals and essays: pleasure at her forward thinking, dismay at her backward thinking, admiration for her writing and painting, amusement at her sense of humor, pain for her pain—sadness that I will not be able to ask her questions, but that's another list—an endless one—the questions. For now I see her as she writes in her "UN-PRIVATE JOURNAL," sitting in the suite of the San Carlos Hotel with her notebook and pencil. Here—she seems to say to me—read this and sort me out—then sort yourself out.

✻

Like my grandmother, I make lists. The exercise is linear, unlike drawing and filling a magic circle with images, yet the act of writing a list gives each item on it a particular power that lingers with a light that shines, whether faint or bright, until a task is fulfilled. Making a list is a way for me to sort myself out. I start my day with a list—things I want to do or accomplish, either during the day or eventually. The items are not in order of importance and can be trivial (clean bathroom) or significant—things that cannot be completed in the course of a morning or one day or even in a year (work on manuscript). The following is typical of my lists, a mix of the small and large in no particular order, but each essential in its own way.

Things My Grandmother Gave To Me and Taught me:

She read to me and taught me how to read.

That one should always try to be kind.

She taught me how to darn socks, a skill I have never needed, thank god, but I am glad to recognize what a darning egg is.

That one should always be respectful and gentle with animals because they know and feel things that we cannot.

To watch out for fairies sleeping under the flowers in the garden.

There are numinous places everywhere.

She sang to me, songs and lullabies that I sang to my own children.

How to play solitaire, and I am addicted to it—as she was.

That the concerns and work of men carried more weight in the world than those of women. Though she never said this to me, it came from one of the voices in her mind, and I learned it; now I continue to un-learn it.

She taught me how to make a good vinaigrette dressing, even though she hated to cook and only made salads and dried-up hamburgers or baked eggs on the cook's days off.

She tried to teach me to paint with watercolors, but I had no patience or talent for it.

She listened.

She taught me to study and listen to people.

That people are both funny and sad—sometimes at the same time.

That organized religion is not all it pretends to be, and faith and belief are two different things.

She explained what a paradox is and showed me how to live it, in it, with it.

She never told me I couldn't do something because I was a girl.

She gave me her gold bracelet with the name "Martha" sculpted into it. I wear it for both of us when I have to present myself to the world as a serious grown-up.

She gave me her mandala.

V
Full Circle

January 1, 1954

There is "a bustle in the house" late on New Year's night in The Acorns. I am awakened by hushed female voices and the sounds of footsteps rushing through hallways and up and down the stairs. The footsteps in the halls are light and quick; on the stairs some are heavy and slow. There are strangers in the house. In between doors closing and opening I hear sobbing and certain words—"gone," "dead."

My grandfather is dead. I know that when living things die, they stop all motion. Something inside them goes away, sometimes suddenly or violently. Last summer, when I was six, I saw three dogs chase a kitten under some blackberry bushes and then tear it apart—a terrible scene that I haven't forgotten. I tried to rescue the kitten but couldn't get past the snarling frenzy of dogs. I could see the mangled kitten, its belly ripped open. My grandmother tried to console me, tried to explain, but it took a long time before I could keep from seeing the bloody images inside my eyelids. And I don't know quite what it means that my grandfather is dead, is gone.

The halls in The Acorns are brown tunnels, the capillaries of the house through which everyone flows. Some lead to light and open rooms, some to hiding places. I run through the brown halls away from my grandparents' bedroom where my grandfather has just died of heart failure. I know his body is there, but I did not see it because we couldn't go in the room. He was sick all through Christmas, though he came downstairs for Christmas morning and dinner. We children didn't understand how sick he was.

My sister is with me. She is frightened and crying, but I drag her along. Aunt Alice has told us to go this way through the halls. At first Aunt Alice was right behind us, and then she turned back toward the room where my grandfather was, his body is. Our mother is somewhere else—in the room? Our grandmother is in the room where the body is.

We pass several doors along the corridor, hesitating at the linen closet, a large space with many shelves stacked with pressed sheets, towels, tablecloths and crocheted doilies. It is a good hiding place with enough space for two of us under the bottom shelf. But we keep going, passing through an entryway three stairs down, to the old servants' quarters—almost empty these days except for Mrs. Wright, the cook. She sleeps there surrounded by the uninhabited bedrooms that line the narrow passage.

I hit my funny bone on the doorframe, collapsing to the floor at the bottom step. For a moment I am paralyzed from the weird sensation in my elbow—as if someone has cut the strings that hold me up. Now my sister and I are both crying. I finally manage to get back up on my feet, my legs like jelly. We move forward through the brown tunnel, past the sewing-room with its ironing board and treadle sewing machine, holding our breath as we pass the bathroom that always smells of old pee. At the end of the hallway on the right, is the one occupied bedroom. The door is ajar. Mrs. Wright is asleep, her red braids, usually coiled around her ears in the daytime, flow unfurled across the white pillow. Her teeth float in a glass of water on the bedside table. During the day, Mrs. Wright is the demon witch of the kitchen, all powerful in her realm, the only place in The Acorns where we children must fawn, placate and obey unconditionally. If we are good, she'll make cake for dessert and tell us stories about Ireland. If we transgress in some unintentional way, we are chased from the kitchen with a whistling birch switch. To witness her in deep sleep while all the commotion of new grief swirls through the house feels alien yet somehow more real and disturbing than the fact of my grandfather's death. She mutters in Gaelic. I wonder if she's dreaming of Ireland and the husband she left behind there. We turn left and take the back stairs up to the third floor to the Narnia room. We call it that because of its closet with a secret door in the back that we cannot open. My sister and I will share a bed in the Narnia room tonight.

✷

I was barely seven when my grandfather died, but I can recall a few very specific images of him, fragments, fleeting sensory impressions of what he looked like, his voice, his presence in the rooms and hallways of The Acorns. He was a large man with thick white hair and a red face—broken veins threaded his cheeks and nose. He always wore a suit and a waistcoat with a pocket for his gold watch and fob. I liked looking at the loop of the gold chain and hearing the thin bell of the watch. In another pocket he usually carried a bird caller, a small metal key-like device inserted into a hollow red wooden tube that chirped like a bird when he twisted the key. He wore spats and walked with a cane from his collection made from different types of wood. The canes were kept in an umbrella stand next to the front door. He smoked a lot, a pipe or Kent cigarettes. He had bad breath.

I remember my grandfather's loud laughter at dinner as he pounded a beer tankard on the big oak table. Though not unkind, he was an intimidating presence. He adored his three daughters, but he was not interested in small children. I don't remember any conversations with him, though I do remember him laughing at something I said. I wondered what was so funny. On the occasions my brother, sister and I visited my grandparents, we were usually kept out of his way so as not to disturb him. We made formal appearances at certain meals. He once roared at me when I was about three or four years old for using the butter knife to butter my bread. I burst into tears while my mother loudly scolded him for making such a fuss over a trifle. "She's just a little girl," I recall her saying. I thought how brave she was to speak that way to my grandfather.

In the years after his death when we lived with my grandmother, my grandfather's things remained in The Acorns and at Martha's Vineyard. My grandmother never found the energy to get rid of any of these artifacts, but she didn't treat them as sacred to his memory either. We were allowed free access to the wall cupboards full of shirts, spats and linen handkerchiefs. The bird caller, the gold watch, and a set of gold cufflinks traveled from bureau drawers to desk cubbyholes around the house. Whoever played with them somehow put them back in places where they would all be re-discovered. Closets in various bedrooms contained his clothing, including two cream-colored linen suits and evening clothes—tuxedo and tails—a paisley silk robe, a crimson velvet smoking jacket, a top hat, a straw boater, wing tip shoes, saddle shoes, patent leather evening slippers with grosgrain bows. Because they were men's clothing and quite large, my sister and I never used them for dress-up, but we loved to take them out to touch and study the rich fabrics. Over the years they became more fragile and dusty, finally dissolving into shreds on their wooden hangers.

The paraphernalia of my grandfather's hobbies were always available for us to use as props or toys. My brother made good use of his fishing tackle and old hunting rifles. His pipe rack held an array of corncobs, briars, and meerschaums that made authentic costume accessories. We liked to examine them and sniff the ancient tobacco smell.

His collection of walking canes would disappear from the umbrella stand in the front hall and turn up throughout the house. We used them for swordfights and magic wands. The shelves and shelves of his books kept the walls and ceilings upright until The Acorns finally disgorged us all out to a world beyond the fragile and artificial grace of the Bacons' literary life and shabby gentility.

Though my memories of him are sparse, over the years I have heard and read the stories and memories of Leonard Bacon, mostly from the women in his family—my aunts, mother, grandmother. He was the center of their universe and the obstacle in their path. He was their passion, their poet, their daddy, and their bad boy as he describes himself in his own books and letters.

By the end of his life, Leonard Bacon's star had faded. He never could nor would make the transition to the evolving style and sensibilities of Modernism. Though he published his *Lusiads* translation in 1950 and continued to write reviews and poems, he had trouble finding a publisher for his poetry. He was sad and continued to drink, overeat and smoke too much. He died at sixty-six of chronic heart failure.

Though it pains me, I have to agree with Randall Jarrell's diagnosis of my grandfather's poetry as being like the appendix, a vestigial organ in the evolution of poetry, "being in the age but not of it." Leonard Bacon was, however, more than "a place-card poet," as his friend Thornton Wilder once unkindly remarked to the composer Alec Wilder. The commitment to formalism was not the problem. Some of his poetry is quite lyrical and lovely, and Jarrell gives him credit for this, but that he seemed oblivious of the changes in attitudes toward other people—women, Jews, different races and ethnicities, the "lower" classes—were founded in the sensibilities of an old order of privilege and the power of the elite. I have found myself cringing at some of his blithely misogynistic and anti-Semitic satirical poems as well as passages in the autobiography, while trying to remind myself that he was a man of a certain time and social order. He did not consciously attack people and would never have admitted to anti-Semitism, racism or sexism; he was not a polemicist or a politically motivated sermonizer, but he assumed his readers would share his perspective of who and what was the natural order, what was inferior or superior. Leonard Bacon's work is more marred by this than by any adherence to rhythm and rhyme.

✳

On the last page of a diary she kept for the year 1953, my grandmother wrote the date, January 1st 1954, and the words "The End." On the line below, "Leonard has gone." The diary for 1953 is only a four-inch book with lined pages, a red plaid cover and a lock without a key. Though not "un-private," it was easily opened with a pair of scissors. Most of the diary's contents were short entries filled with weather reports and health concerns for Leonard and her sister Harriet, whom she and Leonard had been supporting through years of mental and physical illness. My grandmother reported Harriet's death from a stroke that year in October. The other entries were about my mother, Marnie, and her increasingly difficult financial situation—and about my brother and sister and me. The three of us went back and forth between our grandparents' house in 1953 and a place my mother rented in Newport, Rhode Island, while our parents were divorcing. My mother was living with a man whom she would marry before the end of the year. The diary is busy and interesting with our comings and goings, but not reflective as in the earlier long one.

Patty Bacon would not keep a journal in which she fully expressed herself again until 1956, when she started filling another loose-leaf binder with pages of white paper written in pencil. Once again, the title page in large capital letters announced an "UN-PRIVATE JOURNAL—Continued 15 years later."[51] She wrote in this journal on and off until it trickled away in 1964, three years before she died. Its pages are full of sad reflections on illness and contemplations of death, the losses of her husband and sister within months of each other, the severe financial and emotional burden of supporting my mother and her three children through all the feckless choices my mother made. Patty Bacon's disappointment in her own inability to complete the long story she had written and re-written for more than thirty years takes up pages and pages of the journal. Yet for all the melancholy musings in the writing of her later life, she continued to engage in deep and sometimes lively conversation with herself—in her head and on paper. Her voice is alive and strong even in its dark broodings.

October 16th, 1956
Yesterday I took time off from other matters and read from beginning to end the diary that I kept in New York in 1941. I have not felt like keeping a journal since then, and possibly will not wish to go on with this very

long. I cannot tell. There seem to be three reasons for my wanting to make a start. 1. I have been writing constantly for years, but too tightly. I need to get looser. 2. I may discover something in the process or retrieve a number of things that seem to be sinking into a deep blind hole. 3. I am sixty-five years old and sick in mind and soul and body. Perhaps I will really have to find these things or die. At least it is better to try than to go about—drag about—saying to myself, "Why not die?" Already you have lived a longer life than anyone else in your family.

It occurred to me only a few days ago that there is one "something" that I have been trying to record in four different ways—five if you count the paintings—since the beginning of 1923. That "something" seemed to have its beginning in the frightening psychological upset late in 1922 which might have been fatal, but since it was not fatal, the effects were wholly beneficial to put it mildly.

The five different ways she had tried to record the "something" were in the paintings, in a series of essays that she called "philosophical musings," in the "case history" that she burned, the 1941 journal that followed, and finally in the unfinished story or "memoir" she called by several different titles. The second un-private journal is filled with more thoughts and notes for her long story. *I am now in the middle of the second chapter of the eighth version of* Inlandia *or* The River Door. *If it is not the eighth it is the ninth or tenth—I have really lost track of the number of times I have written it through from beginning to end—and how bad all the versions are.* But the journal is full of much more than her writing struggles. *Most of my <u>time</u> has been spent simply living— extraverting—as Jungians say (I am a Jungian I suppose). Family responsibilities, wars, life-breaking wars, illnesses, travel, years of Christmases, etc. etc*

In the many years of writing the second "un-private journal," she raised and supported another family of children, while she tried to write and re-write the story that churned within her. As they came to her, she wrote her reflections on nature, animals, beauty, imagination, genius, death and faith. That she only *supposed* she was a Jungian makes me think she must have shifted away from interpreting life so completely in a Jungian context, or more likely that she had learned to sift what was of value from what was either useless or harmful.

✳

"The way of life writhes like the serpent from right to left and from left to right, from thinking to pleasure and from pleasure to thinking. Thus the serpent is an adversary and a symbol of enmity, but also a wise bridge that connects right and left through longing, much needed by our life."[52]

There it was again—the squeeze—around the top of her head—that's where it would begin. Then it would wrap itself around her neck, writhing down the right side of her body, weaving its way down her arm, wrist and hand, all the way to her foot. It weighed a ton—the boa constrictor. That's what Patty Bacon called it because it writhed and squeezed first in one place then another. The giant serpent had a disconcerting way of seeming to be asleep, and then suddenly—anywhere, anytime—it would wake up and embrace her violently, wrapping around her body with a series of nasty clenches. She knew the probable cause of its existence, a nerve injury associated with brain tumor surgery in 1946. The tumor had been non-malignant and operable, but she had never completely recovered the full use of her right side. Her right foot dragged slightly when she walked, and her hand, though it allowed her to write or type or sew on a button, no longer permitted her to paint or play music. For eleven years now the paints and brushes have been all dried up in her attic studio, her drawings and watercolors packed in portfolios leaning against the wall.

She had gone to a few doctors when the boa constrictor first appeared, but they had no definitive answers. Realizing that it was up to her to wrestle with the beast, she kept away from the doctors after that. She thought she should to try to make friends with it, but it resisted her. Sometimes it was unbearably severe, sometimes negligible. It did not really disable her physically, but when it was very mean and nasty, it disabled her emotionally or psychically, and that in turn made it worse, a vicious cycle. Being busy—too busy even—kept the snake subdued if not dormant. She no longer tried to explain it to anyone because why would they believe such a tale, and mostly because it was a bore.

In the last year, though, it has become worse, much worse, causing frequent severe headaches like a ton of bricks with a spike in the bottom sitting on top of my head and a decided weakness in my right leg and foot. Almost the worst of all is a feeling in the solar plexus. Is it pressure from the snake's embrace? It is not a pain, but a knot, an anguish, part fear, part dismay, part grief. This I know is a very common ailment with no cure for it but work. Yet it makes work difficult, at times impossible. Once recently, I sat down at the typewriter, and the thing tried to stop me from typing. I had a fit of trembling and stiffness and blinding palpitation at the thought of touching the keys. I told myself that if I didn't go on typing I would possibly never be able to sit down at the typewriter again. I went on somehow and manage often now to rattle away on the typewriter for hours at a time. This is what I have to do: keep busy and keep quiet.

✳

Jung's *The Red Book* is full of snakes, with at least ten beautiful serpent illustrations. Some of them are mandalas and others separate paintings, large and small. Much of the text concerns snakes, including dialogue with a female serpent that Jung identifies as his soul in the section called "Mysterium Encounter." The image of the serpent stayed with Jung as he discovered Kundalini Yoga during his travels to India. In Sanskrit, the Kundalini describes an intense form of spiritual energy "coiled" at the base of the spine. In the Kundalini Yoga tradition, enlightenment depends upon drawing the energy up through the body to awaken the seven chakras, or energy centers, to the highest point at the top of the head. This energy is represented by the image of a coiled snake. Jung saw the Kundalini journey to enlightenment through the chakras as a parallel to his theory of individuation in which the individual must pass through different stages of psychic development, a dangerous process that could lead to a "Spiritual Emergency." In *The Red Book*, Jung illustrates in words and visual images his own "emergency" and describes it again in *Memories, Dreams, Reflections*.

The Kundalini Awakening is

> ...a spontaneous, potent inner cleansing, a transformational phenomenon. Some of the possible physical manifestations that could arise in someone going through this process are: general physical weakness or partial paralysis, tremors, shaking, cramping or spasms, headaches, pain in the back, neck, nerve pain in legs and feet, and surges of high vibrational energy. It is an arduous process and involves

far more than physical symptoms....

Initially (and sometimes for many years) most...individuals undergoing involuntary Kundalini awakening have no idea what is actually transpiring in their bodies and psyches....They carry an unnecessary burden of anxiety, confusion and loneliness in the face of this multi-dimensional process. ... Sometimes they feel on the brink of mental collapse.[53]

I have wondered if a Kundalini Awakening or Spiritual Emergency might be what assailed my grandmother forty years before she wrote about her boa constrictor. Perhaps her later symptoms were more than the delayed side effects of her brain surgery. Ultimately, the long story defeated her. Always self-critical in the extreme, she despaired of herself as a writer. *From now on I must keep quiet until I either do it—really do it—or don't do it.* She couldn't do it, but she found another way to work through "the something" when she realized, that her "tidal wave," was a different sort of event currently recognized in the field of psychology as a "psycho-spiritual emergency" that can lead to a spiritual awakening. Under the category of "Religious or Spiritual Problem", the "psycho-spiritual emergency" is included in the DSM. (Diagnostic and Statistical Manual). With the understanding that her experience with "madness was actually a spiritual event,"[54] in 1961 Patty Bacon wrote "The Friend in the Unconscious," a distillation and interpretation above and beyond the case history. This essay is the resolution and synthesis of the darkness, the dreams, and the visions.

When I dreamed of the white flower I was asleep, I was not "in a state." On the contrary, I had managed in a great burst of effort and clear-sightedness, to achieve an honest orientation to myself. The dream waited and then caught me, literally napping. It did not explain itself, it was simply there. It is mystical like physics and chemistry and biology and mathematics; neither orthodox nor unorthodox, nor improbable, nor unusual, nor in any sense unnatural or supernatural. Yet I was so slow to learn that not until after thirty years of strenuous living did I begin to understand what I had seen—truth that was actual life, familiar, even lowly, defenseless, energetic, born to die and live again. I can easily suppose that it is multiplied around the universe in its own richly nourished earth, none the less real for being unprovable—because I have not "lost my faith," I still believe in my experience.

And now it seems to me that all the rest that I have written here can scarcely matter except as it provides an ambience for the one event, which if described in isolation, could have no least resemblance to itself. And indeed, without the surrounding murkiness of sin and error and inadequacy it is non-existent. I mean of course the living flower and I have called it mystical because of its reality and conceivable materiality. By its very nature it is virtually incommunicable, and yet I believe that it is not secretive. On the contrary it is reaching out, it is "clinging heaven by the hems," it is a prayer to us that asks to be answered not—ONCE AND FOR ALL—but again and again and again, as it almost literally comes up for oxygen, often in the most unexpected places.

I cannot think of any of the visions in my waking trance as mystical. They were tremendous dreams, which have been shared by many others. I have come across them in many books. I recognized them in Rembrandt and Fra Angelico and William Blake. I have found them in Pope, in Coleridge, in Yeats, in Plato, in the Old Testament, in poems that are written in our time, even in very recent scientific speculations made public for the benefit of non-scientists. I have found them in Vaughn, in Herbert, in James Joyce—of course I cannot name them all nor explain why it is so to me that some are mystical and others visionary.

Therefore although I understand the true significance of the "fiery moment...once in a lifetime," I know I am not a mystic, because I chose unhesitatingly to draw back, to seal the opening leading to a way of life that could not be my way, though I believed and never felt the need to say, "help Thou my unbelief."

Secretly, but not secretively, I have tried to make my faulty life an answer to that momentary prayer and a perpetual thanksgiving for the Grace.

My grandmother chose to "seal the opening leading to a way of life that could not be [her] way." She chose to renounce that part of herself, the artist in the world she believed herself to be, in order to carry on in the world as a conventional woman who continued to wrestle with her heart's desire, the "darkness" in her spirit. It is difficult for me to reconcile the spiritual awakening, and her sense of integration with the sacrifice she made. I am reminded of Emily Dickinson's wrenching poem "Renunciation is a piercing virtue.—The letting go—A Presence—for an Expectation—Not now..." when I think of what might have been.

But what about the "boa constrictor?" Perhaps it was another phase in a lengthy Kundalini awakening, a spiritual emergency that caused the initial "nervous breakdown" and her later physical and psychic symptoms. I cannot believe that with certainty, but I do know that she was transformed by creating art, first her paintings of mandalas, and later through her writing. These alleviated the pain in her spirit. In a sense, the boa constrictor—her serpent—was not enemy but a "bridge" to her art that, as Jung suggests connected "her right and left through longing," if not for answers, then for signs and patterns.

" For a little Fairy who has no clothes "

MSB, *Fairy Who has no Clothes, Florence Series*, 1928-32.

✳

My grandmother's spiritual life embraced the supernatural without much concern for heirarchies of dieties or their cultural origins. She understood that spirits were real. She came to this somewhat naturally, but Jung reinforced the tendency:

> In 1959, two years before his death, Jung was interviewed for the BBC television programme *Face to Face*. The presenter, John Freeman, asked the elderly sage if he now believed in God. "Now?" Jung replied, paused and smiled. "Difficult to answer. I know. I don't need to believe, I know."[55]

Given the number, variety and general benevolence of the spiritual beings my grandmother invited to inhabit our daily lives, it is not surprising that I was confused about what I learned in the third grade at St. Francis of Assisi School. Our classroom was in the church basement, a dark, chilly space with high, narrow windows near the ceiling. We students looked up from our desks at these lightless slits, dim with grit, or if it rained, smeared with dripping mud. Most days were long slogs through dreary gray arithmetic, penmanship, and grammar lessons taught by nuns quick with a snapping ruler on knuckles out of place on the desk.

I was resigned to my fate, but every so often there were afternoons when we went into the church to sing at a funeral, a diversion from the dreary classroom but an event

MSB, *Duel With a Bee, Florence Series*, 1928-32.

that, as an eight-year-old, I had never experienced. My brother, sister and I did not go to my grandfather's funeral. After the anxious night in the brown halls, my new stepfather whisked us back to New York, where we had been living that year, while my mother stayed in Peace Dale for the service. On the occasions of St. Francis funerals, the elementary school classes took turns by grade to attend and sing an anonymous (to us) soul into purgatory or wherever it was headed. We were a tidy processional of third graders in our school uniforms (all the girls in our required hats), led by nuns upstairs from the basement and outside in order to enter the arched doors of the church's front entrance.

In the brief moments before climbing the steps, I would imagine breaking out of my place in line, pushing past my classmates, flying down the church steps to the sidewalk and disappearing down the street. I could see and feel myself running down the sloping sidewalk and past the seedy buildings of the "Flats" of Peace Dale, until I reached Kingstown Road. Then I would fly past the Hazard Memorial Library, running hard until I reached the dirt road that led to the field below our house and the final, breathless lap through the long scratchy grass bordering the lower lawn of The Acorns. Once I crossed that boundary, I would be safe and free.

I never did make the break from the funeral march except in my imagination—though I longed to. Instead, I stepped over the threshold of the church with everyone else as if no such fantasy had entered my mind. We were never told who had died, but we sang to a coffin that seemed to glide over the shoulders of the pallbearers like a boat in a stream, down the nave, past the pews to the sanctuary where the priest uttered his Latin spells.

The differences between the two universes of school and home could not have been more extreme. The multitude of small gods who populated the Bacon

MSB, *Who Knows?, Florence Series,* 1928-32.

Was I going to prick this bubble too?

MSB, *Pricking the Bubble, Florence Series,* 1928-32.

family pantheon of deities included the Judeo-Christian being with the long white beard, the benign Virgin in her gilt frame (Ave Maria, Gratia Plana) and at Christmas in miniature three dimensional form with her husband, Joseph and their baby Jesus. They came with a cast and crew of shepherds and herd animals, Oriental kings and harp-bearing angels, all members of an elaborate ceramic crèche assembled once a year on the mantelpiece in our living room. The rest of the year, The Olympian gods presided over our intellectual and artistic life pursuits: literature, painting and music with Apollo and the Muses as our chief guides. We worshipped Nature, too. In the woods that surrounded our house and along the nearby beaches, we not only honored nature's power and beauty, we also knew that roaming gods and goddesses, dryads and naiads, fairies and elves hid among tree roots and rolled in on the ocean's waves.

These supernatural beings were mostly benign, though their stories came with enough gore and violence to keep them interesting without being life-threatening—to us. Queen Mab's nightly visits and Puck's mischief explained loss and breakage, bad moods and small miseries such as the flu and scraped knees. The big gods were so busy with their own bad behavior they didn't seem to have much time for our small quarrels and cranky attitudes. I had no fear of Zeus's thunderbolts nor of Apollo's arrows. Perhaps this was because our deepest reverence focused on a human divinity, the family's primary guide to other-worldly spheres, Dr. Jung. I understood early in my childhood that he was the source of all explanations for the miracles and mysteries of the human condition.

The Bacon family fortunes, already precarious when my grandfather died, declined drastically soon afterward. In June of 1954 my family left New York, where we had moved in the fall of 1953, to live with MayMay. This time we stayed for two years. My mother found a job in Boston, where she was a copy editor for *The Atlantic Monthly*. My new (and first) stepfather was writing his never-to-be-published novel in their apartment. They usually traveled home by train on most weekends, but during my mother's interminable weeklong absences, in spite of MayMay's love and attention, I developed a number of neurotic tendencies.

I was terrified my mother was going to die in an accident and that I was suffering from a fatal illness that prevented me from falling asleep. I was sure I would be sick in the night and possibly die while I slept. The family doctor prescribed an emerald green, mint-flavored medicine, which he told me would keep me alive through the night. I believed in the power of this elixir absolutely and could not, would not, sleep without it. I now think it was probably paregoric mixed with a tincture of mint, though the first time I tasted Crème de Menthe I thought I had re-discovered my green medicine. I was addicted to my nightly teaspoon of green sleeping potion; magical thinking has always been helpful to me.

I also dreaded going to school. For some reason, my mother held a strong prejudice against the local public school system, so she had enrolled me at the Catholic elementary school located in the dark, damp basement of St. Francis of Assisi Church. I was outfitted with navy blue uniforms and ugly brown oxford shoes. My brother was shipped off to live in New York, so that he could to go the private school where our father was an art teacher. My sister went to the Catholic kindergarten called The Lily Pads, a somewhat more gentle institution than my school. MayMay cared for us with all her heart. Though she could be a little vague and preoccupied with her writing at times, she helped me to cover my new books in brown paper, made sure my white blouse was pressed and my hair braided every morning before I left for school. She gave me my green medicine and sang my sister and me to sleep at night. These careful gestures weren't enough to protect me.

Before I started school in September, my mother tried to limit the influence of the inevitable religious instruction by meeting with the Mother Superior. They agreed that I would not be required to participate in catechism classes. My mother firmly told me that I should not take part in the lessons, but her efforts at long distance control had no effect at all. I was always in the room during catechism class, exposed to the vivid narrative of Christ's life which was too compelling to resist. I would sit very still, absorbed in the imagery of Christ's passion and suffering for our sins, an irresistible story filled with blood and pain.

Staring up at the crucifix above the blackboard in the classroom, I was fascinated by the nails in Jesus' hands and feet, the crown of thorns and the gash in his side. His blood dripped like black beads falling one by one from the wounds, then disappeared before they reached the gray linoleum floor. The black beads of Sister Elena Mary's rosary trembled at her waist as she, trembling, described Jesus' pain when he dragged the cross through the taunting crowds of Romans. Sister Elena Mary, a bride of Christ with tears streaming down her pale cheeks, would hold her hand up in the air so we could all see the gold wedding band. She told us about her marriage to Jesus, the love that transformed her. And she told us what hell was like—the fires and snakes, the stench, the burning pain from our sins. Through it all, I was transfixed.

The nuns called me "our little Protestant" and made sure that a catechism book was placed on my desk during the afternoon sessions. I knew I was not supposed to look at it, but I did. The spongy cardboard cover of the little black book opened to the startling image of a throbbing sacred heart bound and pierced with thorns, followed by pages of text with black and white illustrations to clarify the lessons. I loved the tiny white bird in flight, the "holy spirit," that flitted through the pages. One picture in particular galvanized me: the human soul appeared in a triptych of cartoon boxes in varying states of sinfulness. The first frame looked like a small glass milk bottle, creamy white for the unblemished soul; then came a speckled bottle for the soul marred with venial sins, while the third box revealed the soul mired in cardinal sin. It was solid black.

I worried about the stains on my own soul. I had recently discovered a word that had great power, though I didn't know what it meant. One of the boys at school got into trouble for shouting the word across the playground during recess as we huddled in the cold corners of the barren yard. Sister Latissia, the nun on yard duty, made a great public display of first dragging the boy away by his ear and then washing his mouth out with red laundry soap. She held him over the big sink in the lunchroom, running water from the blasting faucet as she plunged the bar of soap into his mouth. We all watched as he choked and gagged on the red suds. Then he was suspended from school for a week.

I held the word in my mind, breathing its sounds, forming them silently with my lips and teeth. I breathed the first letter "f," caught the "k" in back of my throat. We students all discussed its meaning at school in whispers, since no one had defined it for us. There was confusion; it seemed this was a word for an unknown, unimaginable act. Was it funny or too hideous to comprehend? Some of us smirked and laughed; some listened with our eyes bugging out; some ran away from the talk.

Words were important in my family—everyone read them, wrote them, looked them up, listened to their sound effects, measured their length and distance. This word was not in any dictionary I consulted. As one genetically disposed toward language, I was determined to understand and test the limits of this new and potent monosyllable. Whom could I ask about this word? It did not seem to be something MayMay would know about. I decided to test it out on Jesus or God, one or the other, or both, to see how he/ they would react. So far, the boy from the playground was still alive, had not been struck dead, even though God had the power—or so the nuns had warned us.

The test I devised for God and/or Jesus was woven into a game of "scotch ball," a ritual that involved a series of twenty different tosses and bounces of a Pensy-Pinky rubber ball, performed in a rigid sequence of difficult maneuvers. If you messed up, you had to go back to the beginning. It was an infuriating game, its tasks beyond my inferior coordination. My opportunities to curse were plentiful. I stationed myself at the far end of our driveway near a stone wall that led into the woods far enough away from the house so that nobody inside could hear or see me. Every time I missed a catch, I would shout the terrible word to the sky—always accompanied by the name of the white-bearded one or his son. I was an eight year old yelling "fuck god" to the sky, betting my life on an immediate reply. I wanted a big voice or a thunderbolt, a clear sign that my blasphemy had offended.

Nothing happened. No sign appeared one way or the other. I was still alive, my flesh uncharred. At dusk I went in to dinner, disappointed but relieved. Later that night, after my dose of green elixir I wondered as I drifted off to sleep if there was a being who cared what an eight-year-old girl shouted at the sky.

Even more distressing than the state of my immortal, milk bottle soul was Sister Latissia, the nun who punished the boy with the word and who also taught third grade arithmetic. She paralyzed me as she traversed the rows of laboring students like a shark in perpetual motion. She had sallow skin and black eyebrows arched over dark eyes receding like two infinite vanishing points into her cavernous wimple. In her presence, numbers shimmered and became distorted in size and shape as if they were under water. They refused to stay in their columns changing their value every time I checked them. When Sister Latissia walked by my desk, she hissed at me as I wore holes in the paper with my eraser.

MSB, *Dark Angel and Sprite*, c. 1940s, courtesy of Anthony Oliver-Smith.

One school morning, I joined MayMay in the dining room. She sat at her accustomed end of the big oval table in the dining room, sipping her coffee with cream. She had finished her daily breakfast—a poached egg with toast and marmalade. I sat in my dark blue serge uniform jumper and white blouse staring with bleak misery into my bowl of sodden corn flakes until MayMay smiled kindly at me and spoke.

"What is this shadow on your face?"

I was considering my demise—disintegration under the caustic gaze of Sister Latissia. Every day I feared that I might be sucked into the wimple where her eyebrows formed a black "V" above her narrowed eyes. Every day I could feel her judgment of my miserable, numerically stupid, sinful soul. How could I trust a greater being that tormented me with arithmetic and this demonic nun? I tried to explain to MayMay about Sister Latissia.

My grandmother put down her coffee cup and looked directly at me. She was silent for a few seconds.

"I doubt if God's most ardent worshippers are his favorite children."

This was puzzling. What did "ardent" mean? Still, the tone of what MayMay said sounded comforting. I understood, in spite of the mysterious word, that Sister Latissia might not be in such good graces with the Lord. I was curious.

"Do you believe that God is real?

A long pause followed. "I don't believe," another pause, "but I have faith."

This statement mystified and troubled me. She was gazing past me toward the opposite end of the dining room table at the empty chair, once my grandfather's place at the table, as if awaiting confirmation of this statement from him - or perhaps his ghost. She continued in her sweet drifty way:

"Faith and belief are opposites, you know. "

I didn't know, except that this was one of her "pairs of opposites" the eight-year-old me didn't comprehend. I wanted a practical application, a concrete example so I could know if I was in trouble or if I could dismiss the white, black and speckled milk bottles in the catechism book. I needed to know before I could banish the specter of Sister Latissia and possibly God. I wanted to return to the Christmas crèche, the Muses, the fairies in the garden and the Olympian Greeks. I understood there would be no definite answer to my question. Whatever they meant, MayMay's words suggested I could accept that somehow everything would be all right.

I never forgot those words, even though I have no recollection of how I endured the rest of third grade. The following year, my mother relented and sent me to the local public school, where my struggles with arithmatic continued to develop into a life-long aversion to and avoidance of math. Without the wrath of Sister Latissia and an angry supreme being, however, I was able to combat my phobia with language and literature—my arsenal of books and imagination.

Over the years, I have returned in my memory to the conversation I had with my grandmother about faith and belief, urging my mind to untangle the verbal knot, so as to hold firmly to the notion that faith is extricable from belief, indeed is its opposite. My grandmother wrestled with this pair of opposites, writing about it often in her journals, using almost the exact words she spoke to me that morning, as well as the following:

> *Faith is so energetic—it crosses a desert, leads us from mirage to mirage, until we reach the place where the mirage becomes real. It is just about the absolute of irrationality!*

Almost sixty years later, I sit in my Vermont kitchen at the oak table that once occupied the dining room of my grandmother's house. I have taken out all its leaves, so the table, a diminished circle, can fit into the small dining area of my small house. I can still easily conjure the table in the grand dining room of The Acorns, its sturdy fluted legs supporting the heavy top, covered with a damask cloth on holidays, set with the good silver and gold-rimmed china, or on ordinary days with chipped plates and placemats. On one of those ordinary days in the middle of the week, my grandmother explained faith and belief to me as we sat at this table. The brief exchange would set me on a lifelong path of hopeful skepticism, a stage, possibly, on the way to faith—if I can keep following my own mirages.

✳

John Donne Gives Me a Home Thought
Leonard Bacon

It's thirty miles from the Industrial Trust
To "The Acorns." Oh, I know that highroad well.
Ten miles of town, and then the open fell
Where bloom wild roses, or the aureate rust
Of Autumn gleams, snows linger, or leaves thrust,
All in good time. I know the feel and smell
Of exquisite changes that exert a spell
Which always has possessed me, and always must.

The Gods are there. They walk within my woods.
I people all the wilderness with sweet
Phantoms, whose pulses in the dogwood beat,
Lares that watch my hearth, presences felt,
Some influence that in the thicket broods,
And into which making no noise, I melt.[56]

My grandfather's poem takes him home, out of the city, away from the "Industrial Trust," an image laden with urban and commercial irony, and into the idyllic, pastoral place, The Acorns, that "exert[s] a spell which has always possessed [him.]" I can identify with his feelings; just remembering the place "exerts a spell which always has possessed me and always must." Though I am critical of Leonard Bacon as a poet and as a man, my heart and spirit are with him here and in his life story. I wish I had known him better. We called him "Bampa," but the child's nickname did not suit him and is not how I think of him. He did not play the grandpa, "Bampa," role.

I am glad for the poem to take me back to The Acorns. I often return there in impossible fantasies. One of them is that I'll one day be able to buy the house and live in it. It has recently sold again after being on the market for almost two years. The first asking price of $1.8 million gradually fell to around $950,000—hopelessly out of my range. During that time, I kept checking on the status of the sale and taking the online virtual tour of the house, an experience that was so disorienting it gave me vertigo.

I discovered through informants, old friends in Peace Dale, that the last owner/seller of The Acorns was a retired computer scientist and game designer, the current era's equivalent of 19th century industrial magnates like the Hazards who built and lived in such places. He spared no expense on the improvements and enhancements to his Victorian mansion.

Over the years, different owners, or alien invaders, as I sometimes think of them have altered the place. The grounds, my grandfather's "thickets," have been turned into a mini-Versailles with fountains and a large wrought-iron gate, presumably to keep the peasants out. The surrounding woods once full of his "phantoms" were long ago transformed into a housing development crammed with both custom-built houses and tract homes.

The virtual tour revealed that the inside has been remodeled almost beyond recognition. The living room looked like a doctor's waiting room, and the old kitchen had been reincarnated into a gleaming space station attached to a whole new dining room with a marble floor. The dining room was transformed into a "family media center" with a television screen the size of Texas hovering at one end. So much for the "Lares" that watched my grandfather's hearth.

Of course I knew the place would be different after so many years and people making changes. The Acorns has been improved from a falling down wreak to a state of the art, top-of-the-line piece of real estate. I used to imagine that a Mafia boss, a hedge fund manager, or an arts foundation would buy the house and hire me as a docent or a greeter—a summer housekeeper? I like to think that current and future residents, whoever they are, will sometimes pause, imagining they hear among the odd sounds, faint echoes in walls, dark hallways and hidden spaces of the house, the old generations of the Bacon family. I may have haunted the place on a virtual tour, but I will always dwell there, possessed by the lives and stories in a house that no longer belongs to me in reality.

I have fewer fantasies about buying the house these days. Even if I had the outlandish sum of the reduced price, what would I do with such an enormous place? Whoever owns the house now must in these economic times possess an income large enough to afford not only the price but also the upkeep and taxes. My children have no connection to The Acorns—they are all adults—and westerners besides. My New England roots seem quaint and remote to them. My life these days has little connection with that old world of the Hazards and Bacons, a genteel world that no longer exists. I now live in northern Vermont in a small house with a few relics from The Acorns as reminders of my own past and of an era long past.

✹

In my dream, I am in the basement of The Acorns, navigating the labyrinth of rooms that lie beneath the three stories above. All the basement rooms have had specific purposes over the years, but the boundaries have become permeable, their contents flowing into each other's spaces. Dusty wine bottles, still full of wine or whatever it has become, mowers, scythes, saws, drills and blades of various lethal sizes and shapes fill shelves, line walls and workbenches. Stacks of my father's paintings, now rotting canvasses, and damp cardboard boxes filled with manuscripts and mildewed photographs stuck together, turn up everywhere, including the laundry room with its ancient mangle, zinc tubs and shelves of corroded jars stained with the residue of toxic cleaning chemicals. The bomb shelter, a grey concrete cell my mother had installed in the 1950s, contains nothing but the chill of its own dead air. Wooden crates and cast-off furniture, including my mother's blue silk Queen Anne sofa with the cigarette burn on the seat, occupy one room with a stage once used for long-ago family theatrical performances. Solitary and exposed in a doorless recess stands an old toilet with a pull chain. Doors on electrical boxes hang open, revealing rows of dead switches. Plumbing and radiator pipes, strung with spider webs, wind like bulging intestines along walls and up through ceilings.

I find myself in the basement's central chamber where I face the furnace, a huge prehistoric creature with octopus-tentacle ducts that reach above its massive galvanized hulk. The furnace was my grandmother's enemy for years. Every winter night she descended into the basement, a small, tremulous warrior, to negotiate with the irascible beast, coaxing, willing its gauges and pilot light to relinquish heat for yet another day. In my dream, I stare into the opening in the cast iron hatch, a tiny pug-nose door on its swollen face. Nothing but darkness—the beast is extinct.

But now a man in uniform, white-billed cap, epaulets on his blue jacket, stands before me, the captain of an ocean liner docked in the space where the furnace had been. There is a gangplank that I must cross in order to board the ship about to leave the harbor on a voyage. My grandmother stands beside the captain. She tells me that I must get my papers in order—I can't board until they are ready.

✳

My boarding papers—the journals, letters, lists, essays, stories—are strewn about my office along with stacks of paintings, drawings, Bacon family photographs and my mandala. I cannot say they are in order for my dream's voyage, wherever that might take me. I know enough of what's in them to say that I've told a piece of my own story, ninety degrees, perhaps, of the circle. But I trust that my grandmother's instructions are important to follow if I'm to sort out the next turn of the story's wheel.

Faith is so energetic—it crosses a desert, leads us from mirage to mirage, until we reach the place where the mirage becomes real. It is just about the absolute of irrationality!

When does the mirage become real? I like to think that when MayMay gave her mandala to a rebellious, pregnant teenage girl as we stood together in her attic studio in The Acorns on the day of my wedding, she was committing an act that was the "absolute of irrationality"—an act of faith. She had faith that I would be worthy of her gift—that someday I would find and read her words, that I would take her paintings and her story out of the darkness she believed she was destined as a woman to inhabit, to a place where they can shimmer in the light.

MSB, Illustration for an essay on Time, 1930s.

Notes

1. Martha Stringham Bacon, "The Friend in the Unconscious" (unpublished essay, 1961, Bacon Family Archives).

2. Carl Gustav Jung, *Modern Man in Search of a Soul* (1933; repr., London: Routledge & Kegan Paul, 2003), 175.

3. Martha Stringham Bacon, *Martha Stringham Bacon, "Time II: Thirteen O'Clock" (unpublished essay, 1956, Bacon Family Archives), 4.*

4. Leonard Bacon, *Semi-Centennial: Some of the Life and Part of the Opinions of Leonard Bacon* (New York: Harper & Brothers, 1939), 69.

5. "Irving Stringham," Wikipedia, last modified August 13, 2013. http://en.wikipedia.org/wiki/Irving_Stringham

6. Frederick Faust, friend and student of LB at the University of California at Berkeley. He was an author whose penname was Max Brand. His works include *Destry Rides Again* and the *Dr. Kildare* series.

7. Martha Stringham Bacon to Helen Bacon, 1 October 1949, Bacon Family Archives.

8. Leonard Bacon, *Semi-Centennial*, 171.

9. Ibid.,172

10. Ibid.,177

11. Leonard Bacon to Chauncy and Henriette Goodricch, 25 June 1925 in Chauncey S. Goodrich, "Transatlantic Dispatches From and About Zurich," *Spring: An Annual of Archetypal Psychology and Jungian Thought* (offprint; Dallas: Spring Publications, 1983).

12. Leonard Bacon, "Mnemonic System for Psycho-analysts," *Rhyme and Punishment* (NewYork: Farrar and Rhinehart, 1936), 10.

13. In the dedication to *Semi-Centennial*, LB refers to John Donne with the assumption that his wife and daughters and perhaps his readers know what he is alluding to. At this point, the search for clues about the allusion continues. LB also titled one of his own poems "John Donne Gives Me a Home Thought," which is presented in Chapter V.

14. Leonard Bacon, *Semi-Centennial*, 177

15. Martha Stringham Bacon to Helen Hazard Bacon, undated, Yale Collection of American Literature, Beinecke Rare Book and Manuscript Library, Yale University. The letter was written on stationery from the El Encanto Hotel and Bungalows in Santa Barbara, CA. The El Encanto was located near "Dial House," owned by Leonard's Aunt Caroline Hazard. Patty was attended by her own private "strict, nice nurse," who was "beginning to look at [her] suspiciously" as she wrote this letter.

16. Martha Stringham Bacon, "Time I: Morning's at Seven" (unpublished essay, Bacon Family Archives), 4-7.

17. Martha Stringham Bacon, "The Friend in the Unconscious." Much of the material in Chapters II and III is paraphrased or summarized from the essay. Places and sections that are in italics are taken verbatim from the essay. In other segments I have replaced the pronoun "I" with she and use my grandmother's words interspersed with my own interpretations.

18. Leonard Bacon, "Poem XXVII," *Animula Vagula* (New York: Harper & Brothers, 1926), 36.

19. Zelda Fitzgerald accused her husband F. Scott Fitzgerald of plagiarizing her life after he used their personal story and her diaries in his work. Zelda, also a writer, tried to become a dancer in her late twenties but

suffered a mental breakdown from which she never recovered. She was committed to an asylum and died there after seventeen years. Dorothy Wordsworth's *Grasmere Journals* became the source material for many of her brother's poems. She recorded scenes in nature that Wordsworth "recollected in tranquility." The brother and sister were extremely close, but when he married, Dorothy lost her mind. She apparently recovered only after her brother's death when she was in her eighties.

20. Martha Stringam Bacon, journal entry, March, 1927, Bacon Family Archives.

21. Laurie Lisle, *Portrait of an Artist: A Biography of Georgia O'Keeffe* (New York: Washington Square Press, 1997), 264.

22. Ibid., 42.

23. Ibid., 157.

24. Martha Stringham Bacon, "Sun in a Trap" (unpublished essay, undated, Bacon Family Archives), 10.

25. Jung, *Modern Man in Search of a Soul,* 175.

26. Martha Stringham Bacon to her three daughters, June 1927 (Bacon Family Archives).

27. Martha Stringham Bacon to her daughter Marnie Bacon, 6 May, 1927 (Bacon Family Archives).

28. Leonard Bacon, *Semi-Centennial*, 178.

29. Deirdre Bair, *Jung: A Biography* (New York: Little Brown, 2003. For further information about Jung's life and work, see Frank McClynn, *Carl Gustav Jung* (New York: St. Martin's Press, 1997).

30. Leonard Bacon, *Semi-Centennial*, 181.

31. Rowland Hazard, LB's cousin, was treated unsuccessfully by Jung. Hazard eventually connected with Bill Wilson through Jung's recommendation and was instrumental in the foundation of Alcoholics Anonymous. For further information, see Claire Dunne, *Wounded Healer of the Soul* (New York: Parabola, 2000).

32. Carl Jung, to Leonard Bacon, 19 November, 1932, Yale Collection of American Literature, Beinecke Rare Book and Manuscript Library, Yale University. The book Jung refers to might have been *Lost Buffalo and Other Poems*, published in 1930.

33. Carl Jung, to Leonard Bacon, 20 September, 1928, Yale Collection of American Literature, Beinecke Rare Book and Manuscript Library, Yale University.

34. C.G. Jung, *The Red Book: Liber Novus*, ed., Sonu Shamdasani (New York: Norton, 2009), inside and back cover quotation.

35. Carl Jung to Martha Stringham Bacon, 27 October, 1932, Bacon Family Archives.

36. Martha Stringham Bacon, to Carl Jung, unsent and undated, probably sometime late in 1932, in response to his 1932 letter about photographs of the mandala paintings she sent to him, Bacon Family Archives.

37. Martha Stringham Bacon excerpts from 1936 journal, Bacon Family Archives.

38. All direct quotations from MSB's notes taken during Jung's visit appear in italics.

39. Leonard Bacon to Chauncy Goodrich, 10 May, 1925, in which Leonard describes his Zurich adventures, in Goodrich "Transatlantic Dispatches."

40. C.G. Jung to Heinrich Zimmer, 14 December 1936, in *C.G. Jung Letters: Vol 1, 1906-1950*, ed. Gerhard Adler and Aniela Jaffe (London: Routledge & Kegan Paul, 1973), 223.

41. Randall Jarrell, "Poets: Old, New and Aging," *Kipling, Auden and Company: Essays and Reviews, 1935-1964* (New York: Farrar Straus and Giroux, 1980), 41-51.

42. Leonard Bacon, "Defense of Poetry," *Semi-Centennial,* 249-273

43. Toni Wolff to Leonard Bacon, 21 March, 1933, Yale Collection of American Literature, Beinecke Rare Book and Manuscript Library, Yale University.

44. Toni Wolff to Leonard Bacon, 20 February, 1937, Yale Collection of American Literature, Beinecke Rare Book and Manuscript Library, Yale University.

45. Toni Wolff to Leonard Bacon, 29 February, 1937, Yale Collection of American Literature, Beinecke Rare Book and Manuscript Library, Yale University.

46. Leonard Bacon, to Helen Bacon, December, 1940, Bacon Family Archives.

47. Throughout the war, my grandmother sent packages to Stoker Jack Jones as well as to another POW soldier named Basil Gunnell. Each sent her many thank you notes and cards from their POW camps on the official German "Postkartes" and the folded stationery allotted to them. Stoker Jones sent her a group photo of himself with his barrack mates. His parents also wrote to her.

48. Martha Stringham Bacon, material from chapter IV excerpted and paraphrased from "An Un-Private Journal," 1941, Bacon Family Archives.

49. Martha Stringham Bacon, "Sun in a Trap" (unpublished essay, undated, Bacon Family Archives).

50. Claire Douglas, *The Woman In The Mirror* (Boston: Sigo Press, 1990), 61.

51. Quoted passages, summaries and paraphrases from Martha Stringham Bacon, "An Un-Private Journal: Continued 15 Years Later," Bacon Family Archives.

52. Jung, *The Red Book*, 247.

53. El Collie, "Mysteries of the Goddess," in Shared Transformation, accessed June 12, 2014, http://www.kundaliniawakeningsystems1.com/downloads/branded-by-the-spirit_by-el-collie.pdf.

54. Darlene B, Viggiano and Stanley Krippner, "The Grof's Model of Spiritual Emergency in Retrospect: Has it Stood the Test of Time?" *International Journal of Transpersonal Studies,* 29, no. 1, (2010) : 118-127.

55. Mark Vernon, *Face to Face* interview, BBC TV. Guardian.co. uk. Monday, 18 July, 2011.

56. Leonard Bacon, "John Donne Gives Me a Home Thought," *Yale Literary Magazine* 104 (1932): 30.

MARTHA OLIVER-SMITH was born in Peace Dale, Rhode Island in 1946 to a family of writers, artists and scholars. She spent most of her childhood moving between her grandmother's home in Peace Dale and living with her mother in New York. She moved west with her young family in 1972 to Ashland, Oregon where she completed a BA in English from Southern Oregon University. In 1976, she moved to Reno, Nevada to earn an MA in English literature from the University of Nevada where she began her thirty-six year teaching career. After twenty-five years of teaching college and high school literature and writing courses in Oregon, Nevada and California, Oliver-Smith moved back east to Vermont in 2002 to teach and to research and write *Martha's Mandala*. In 2006, she earned an MFA in creative writing from Vermont College of Fine Arts where her thesis provided the basis for the memoir. She lives with her husband, two cats, one dog and six chickens in northern Vermont where she is working on a second memoir.

41905535R00090

Made in the USA
Charleston, SC
12 May 2015